INVESTING ON THE AUSTRALIAN SHAREMARKET

SUN

INVESTING ON THE AUSTRALIAN SHAREMARKET

M.J. AITKEN A.W. BURROWES R.D. MULHOLLAND

Copyright © M.J. Aitken, ISAD Trust, R.D. Mulholland 1983

First published by Sun Books 1983
THE MACMILLAN COMPANY OF AUSTRALIA PTY LTD
107 Moray Street, South Melbourne 3205
6 Clarke Street, Crows Nest 2065

Associated companies and representatives
throughout the world

Reprinted 1986 (twice), 1987, 1988 (twice)

National Library of Australia
cataloguing in publication data

Aitken, M.J.
   Investing on the Australian sharemarket.

   ISBN 0 7251 0414 7.

   1. Stock-exchange —Australia 2. Investments —
Australia. I. Burrowes, A.W. (Ashley W.).
II. Mulholland, R.D. (Raymond D.). III. Title.

332.64'2'94

Set in Century Schoolbook by Savage & Co., Brisbane
Printed in Hong Kong

This book is sold subject to the condition that it shall not, by
way of trade or otherwise, be lent, re-sold, hired out, or
otherwise circulated without the publisher's prior consent in
any form of binding or cover other than that in which it is
published and without a similar condition including this
condition being imposed on the subsequent purchaser.

Contents

List of Figures	xi
Preface	xii
Acknowledgements	xiii

1. **INTRODUCTION**   1
   - Financial Assets   2
     1. Company shares   2
     2. Fixed-term securities   2
   - Advantages of Financial Assets   3
   - Trading in Financial Assets   4

2. **COMPANIES AND COMPANY SECURITIES**   6
   - Company Structure   6
   - Shares and Capital   7
   - Ordinary Shares   8
   - Preference Shares (old style)   8
   - Convertible Specified Preference Shares (new style)   9
   - Deferred Dividend Shares   10
   - Timing of Dividend Payments   11
   - Dividend Amount   11
   - The Dividend Yield on Shares   11

3. **THE ISSUE OF SHARES**   13
   - Prospectus   13
   - Investing in a New Issue of Shares   15
   - Allotment   15
   - Calls   16
   - The Premium on Shares   16

	Rights Issue of Shares	17
	Renounceable Rights Issue	18
	Non-renounceable Rights Issue	18
	Bonus Issues of Shares	19
4.	THE ISSUE OF DEBENTURE STOCK	21
	Application	21
	Debenture Security	22
	Comparison of Shareholders and Debenture-holders in Relation to the Company	22
	1. Rights of membership	22
	2. Investment return	23
	Other Debenture-issuing Bodies	24
5.	SHARE AND DEBENTURE CERTIFICATES	25
	Share Certificates	25
	Share Registrars	26
	Debenture Securities Certificates	26
6.	THE SHAREMARKET, INVESTORS, AND BROKERS	27
	The Australian Stock Exchange	27
	Listing on the Stock Exchange	27
	The Marketable Parcel and Odd Lots	29
	Trading on the Floor of the Exchange	29
	Profile of Investors	30
	Sharebrokers and Their Activities	31
	The Transfer of Shares	32
7.	INVESTMENT DECISIONS ON THE SHAREMARKET	34
	The Required Psychological Profile	34
	Share Trading to Beat Inflation	35
	Macro-economic Factors Affecting the Sharemarket	36
	Economic Forces Influencing Sectors of the Market or Individual Companies	39
	1. Company management	40
	2. Company diversification	40
	General	41

8.	**SELECTING SHARES**	42
	Market Leaders	42
	Choosing Shares	43
	Share price	43
	Bonus issues	43
	Rights issues	44
	Dividends	44
	Marketability	44
	Security	45
	Financial soundness	45
	The Portfolio	46
9.	**SHARE PURCHASE STRATEGY**	48
	Ups and Downs in the Market	48
	Glamour Shares — the Underpriced and the Overpriced Share	49
	Long-term or Short-term Investing?	49
	Purchasing and Taking Up Rights	50
	Calculating the Price of a Right	51
	Trading in Rights	52
	Investing in an Initial Flotation	52
	Investing in Convertible Notes and Shares	53
10.	**INVESTMENT ANALYSIS: 1**	55
	Fundamental Analysis	55
	1. Earnings per share (EPS)	56
	2. Price/earnings ratio (P/E ratio)	56
	3. Dividend per share (DPS)	57
	4. Dividend yield	58
	5. Times dividend covered	59
	6. Net tangible asset backing (NTA)	60
	General	60
11.	**INVESTMENT ANALYSIS: 2**	62
	Technical Investment Strategy	62
	Tools of the Technician	62
	Charting	63
	1. Point-and-figure charting	63
	2. Bar charting	66
	Mechanical Rules	68
	Summary	68

12.	**SHAREMARKET INDICES**	70
	Introduction	70
	Objective of Share Price Indices	70
	1. Selection of companies	71
	2. Weighting	72
	3. Method of averaging	72
	Australian Share Price Indices	73
	Frequency of calculation	75
	ASE Index Sampling, Weighting, and Averaging	76
	1. Sample	76
	2. Weighting and averaging	76
	Other Stock Exchange Indices	77
	Some Selected Overseas Indices	77
	1. The Dow Jones industrial average	77
	2. Standard and Poor's index	78
	3. *Financial Times* index	78
	4. *Financial Times* — actuaries' index	78
	Conclusion	78
13.	**UNDERSTANDING ANNUAL ACCOUNTS**	80
	Balance Sheet	81
	Balance Sheet Preparation	81
	The Tie Between the Balance Sheet and the Profit-and-loss Statement	82
	Profit-and-loss Statement	82
	The Directors' Report	83
	The Auditors' Report	83
	Funds Statements	83
	Trend Statements	84
	Accounting Jargon	84
14.	**INVESTING IN FIXED-TERM SECURITIES**	85
	Fixed-term Investing	85
	Authorities Issuing Fixed-term Securities	85
	1. Commonwealth government	85
	2. Semi-government authorities	87
	3. Business organizations	88
	The Term and Rate of Interest	88

	The Sale of Fixed-term Securities	90
	Very-short-term Investing	91
	Cash Management Trusts	91
	Mortgage Investing	92
15.	THE AUSTRALIAN OPTIONS MARKET	93
	Put and Call Options Trading on the Australian Options Market	94
	Reasons for Purchasing Call Options	95
	Reasons for Purchasing Put Options	96
	Selling Both Call and Put Options	97
	Reasons for Selling Call Options	97
	Reasons for Selling Put Options	99
	Additional Strategies	100
	1. Buying a straddle	100
	2. Writing a straddle	100
	Summary	101
16.	TAXATION	102
17.	SOURCES OF INFORMATION	104
	Instantaneous Information	104
	1. On-line Share Price Indices	104
	2. Stockbrokers (sharebrokers)	105
	Daily Information	105
	Daily Diary	105
	Weekly Information	106
	Weekly Diary	106
	Monthly Information	107
	Australian Stock Exchange Journal	107
	Comparative Analysis	107
	Annual Information	108
	Stock Exchange Research Handbook	108
	Financial and Profitability Study	108
	Company Profit Announcements	108
	Stock Exchange Statex Service	108
	Australian Business Profitability	109
	Jobson Year Book	109
	Company annual and interim reports	109
	Other Publications	110
	Periodic Information	110

	Sharebrokers' newsletters	110
	Investment letters	111
	Forecasting letters	111
	Business journals	111
	Stock exchange investment service	111
	Comment	112
18.	DEALING WITH BROKERS	113
	Choosing a Broker	113
	Making the Best Use of a Broker	114

Appendix A. Brokerage Rates	116
Appendix B. Glossary of Sharemarket Terms	119
Appendix C. Radio Australia Broadcasts, Stock Exchange Broadcasts, and Stock Exchange Telephone Service	132

List of Figures

	page
1. ASE All Ordinaries Price Index	64
2. Point-and-figure Charting with Time Dimension	65
3. Bar Charting	66
4. Five Standard Chart Patterns	67

Preface

This book is intended to be a simple introduction to the Australian sharemarket for those who have little or no knowledge of its workings. In clear terms it outlines the different opportunities for investment and the factors that must be taken into account when choosing one investment alternative over another.

It defines what the relationship is between the stock exchange, the companies and organizations offering financial securities, the stockbroker, and the would-be investor. It informs the reader how to find out about investment prospects, how to chart the progress of investments, and how and when to buy and sell. It describes what the investor can and should do for himself, and when he should seek professional assistance, and where to locate that assistance, whether it is in the form of personal advice or publications.

Although most forms of exchange traded are discussed, the largest amount of space is devoted to public company securities, especially shares, for these make up the bulk of securities traded on the stock exchange.

Although some companies and organizations are mentioned in this book, that is not to be interpreted as constituting advice about particular investments.

M. J. AITKEN

Acknowledgements

We wish to acknowledge the assistance of the Investor Services section of the Sydney Stock Exchange, and, in particular, Mr Paul Pinnock, who provided invaluable assistance during the writing of this book. We also gratefully acknowledge the assistance of Mr Peter Small, Manager of the Options Clearing House, who allowed us to use material originally written by him, in the construction of chapter fifteen.

A vital contribution was made by Trisha Todd, who made innumerable contributions to the style and organization of the book.

While the authors recognize the help given by others, they accept ultimate responsibility for the published text.

M.J.A., A.W.B., R.D.M.

Chapter One
Introduction

Any person with surplus cash in hand can use this cash to acquire additional income. There are two broad options available to him. In the first instance he may use the money to purchase all or part of the assets of an existing or newly created business. The alternative is to place his funds at the disposal of government, semi-government, or business organizations, by purchasing the securities (financial assets) of any of these bodies. The basic difference between these investment alternatives is that in the first instance the investor actually owns the assets of the business, whereas in the other he owns only a piece of paper — a bond or debenture deed, which entitles him to a fixed rate of interest, or a share certificate which entitles him to a share in the profits, if any, of the business.

If a person decides to use his money to purchase a business, either as sole proprietor or as a partner, he will find that the rewards can be great, but so too can be the risks. If a business fails, creditors can make claim on all personal assets of the owner or partners, irrespective of whether they were intended to be part of the business or not. This may, for example, include the house that he and his family live in. In addition to these risks, there is the fact that this type of investment requires the constant personal attention of the investor as well as the appropriate expertise. He may also have to raise additional finance in the form of a loan to supplement his resources.

If the investor does not want to take these risks, or give his investments his undivided attention, then the alternative of investing in financial assets gives him the opportunity to gain additional income while pursuing his normal interests or profession.

Financial Assets

Financial assets may be broadly divided into two categories: company shares and fixed-term securities.

1. *Company Shares*
In physical terms little more than pieces of paper with writing on them, company shares are exchanged for an investor's money, which in turn constitutes the basic working capital of a company. Such a share entitles the holder to receive some proportion (depending on the amount of shares held) of the profit of a business. A characteristic that distinguishes shares from fixed-term securities is that, except in very rare cases (explained later), shares do not mature. The money initially outlayed in their purchase is not returned to the shareholder either at a predetermined date or, indeed, at any other time unless the company goes into liquidation. The only means available to an investor to liquidate his investment is to sell his shares through an organized market (the stock exchange) to anyone interested in buying them.

2. *Fixed-term Securities*
These are securities that mature after a specified period of time. In this type of investment, the capital sum spent to purchase them is repaid to the particular person who holds the security at the date it matures. Such securities can include semi-government securities, debenture stock, unsecured notes, fixed-term savings accounts, and first mortgage contracts. A variety of organizations may issue fixed-term securities. All manner of state authorities — including electricity, water, and gas boards — can issue semi-government securities. Similarly, all sorts of limited liability companies can issue debenture stock and/or unsecured notes. In the case of

fixed-term savings accounts, these can be placed with trading banks, building societies, or credit unions. First mortgages, which are loans secured by a charge over property owned by the borrower, are something of an exception. They can be arranged only through a solicitor.

Two other forms of investment that may be regarded as fixed-term securities include treasury notes and endowment insurance policies. In respect of the former, if an investor has a significant sum of money that he wishes to invest over a short period, say 180–190 days, he may make use of what is known as the short-term money market and purchase a treasury note from the federal government.

Endowment insurance policies are issued by most insurance companies. In this instance, though, the contract concluded between the insured and the insurance company and the power to 'deal' in the policy is very limited. Endowment insurance policies cannot be bought and sold the way other securities can, and it is usually taken out to provide financial security to the person insured rather than as an income-earning investment. In this respect, although the insurance company may declare bonuses on the policy, the return is usually less than that paid on other fixed-term securities.

Advantages of Financial Assets

The primary advantage of placing funds in assets such as company shares or fixed-term securities as against purchasing a business is that once the initial investment (placement of funds) has been made, less personal attention and little in the way of technical expertise is required from the investor. The investor is then able to devote himself to other activities, which may include pursuing a particular vocation or simply enjoying retirement. At the same time, the risks the investor carries with such investment are comparatively negligible, provided that a reasonable degree of discretion has been exercised in making the investment. On this last point it should be noted that there are considerable differences (which will be discussed later in more detail) between the various types of financial assets, and some are more suitable for different categories of investors than others. Accepting this qualification, however, financial assets provide a very effective form of investment for people interested in pursuing other occupations and for retired persons who want to limit their personal and/or financial commitment and responsibility in the pursuit of additional income.

Trading in Financial Assets

Trading in financial assets is not something that can be done at any time, at any place, and by any person. Financial assets are normally traded only through an organized market, known as the stockmarket. This market is conducted between the hours of 10 a.m. and 12 p.m. and 2 p.m. and 3 p.m. each working day. It is conducted on behalf of investors by accredited brokers in one of the six stock exchanges throughout Australia. The basic function of a stock exchange is to act as a financial intermediary in raising business funds. In performing this function it fulfils the needs of two parties: on the one hand, business organizations that need funds to operate, and, on the other, the investor who is looking to invest his surplus money. The following constitutes a list of securities that are regularly traded on the exchange.
1. Ordinary Shares.
2. Semi-government fixed-interest loan securities. By semi-government we mean organizations such as the Department of Main Roads and the various state electricity bodies.
3. Loan securities of finance companies.
4. Company loan securities.
5. Options.
6. Preference shares.
7. Unsecured convertible notes.

This list is arranged in order of the frequency with which

securities are traded. For explanations of unfamiliar terms, refer to Appendix B. Although most of the securities traded on the stock exchange are dealt with in this book, priority is given to explaining company financial assets because investment in these securities far outweighs investment in other types of securities.

Chapter Two
Companies and Company Securities

The shares bought and sold on the stock exchange will, in the main, have been issued by limited liability companies, as will a substantial volume of fixed-term securities. Thus companies feature both as borrowers in the investment arena and as the source of securities that change hands on the stockmarket. Some knowledge of their structure, legal basis, and mode of operation is therefore essential to investors.

Company Structure

A company is a business entity, formed for the purpose of making a financial profit. Companies are controlled legally by the Companies Act 1981 (Commonwealth). Although the Act exerts a tight general control over the activities of companies, they are still accorded a considerable degree of freedom to conduct their own affairs. These affairs must, however, be carried out within the broad framework of the legislation.

The Act provides that a company must be registered with the appropriate State Corporate Affairs Commission. Until it is so registered, it cannot commence business. Once registered, the company assumes a corporate identity separate from the actual individuals who comprise its board of directors, staff, or shareholders. One of the consequences of this is that companies are taxed in their own right at different rates from those of individuals. (See Chapter 16.)

A company must file among its registered documents a memorandum and articles of association. These set out the purpose and powers of the company and the manner in which the internal business of the company is to be conducted. The company must at all times act in accordance with the provisions of these two documents, otherwise its activities will be *ultra vires* and of no effect. The business of the company in respect of policy matters is conducted by means of resolutions. For most routine matters ordinary resolutions will suffice, but for matters such as alteration of the articles or memorandum, it will be necessary for the company to pass a special resolution at a general meeting. The shareholders will be given prior notice of this. Such resolutions will generally be required for new issues of shares or the raising of debenture finance. Each public company is required to convene an annual general meeting where shareholders are entitled to question management about the financial policies of the organization. At this meeting it is within the power of shareholders to remove management.

Shares and Capital

Any company will require a certain amount of capital with which to commence business. The capital of the company must be set out in the memorandum of association. The capital will be divided into shares, and the manner in which it is so divided must also be included in the memorandum. The shares will normally be of either 50 cents or $1 nominal value. Most shares in Australia are now of 50 cents nominal value, following the tendency over the past few years for companies with $1 shares to split them into 50 cent shares, because the smaller value units tend to negotiate more readily on the sharemarket. Some companies have shares whose par value is less than and sometimes greater than 50 cents.

Shares may assume a number of different forms and have different 'incidents', that is, rights and obligations attached to them. The different categories of shares more commonly found in Australia will now be considered.

Ordinary Shares

Ordinary shares form by far the greater portion of the capital of Australian companies and are the bulk of the shares that are traded on the stock exchange. They also carry the greatest risk to the shareholder as there are no privileges attached to them in the event of the company going into liquidation. However, ordinary shares usually carry the right to vote at company meetings and to benefit from an upward adjustment of dividends as a result of an increase in company profits. The ordinary shareholder will generally participate in bonus issues of shares, a right that either does not usually attach at all, or attach immediately, to other classes of shares.

Preference Shares (old style)

Preference shares have specific privileges attached to them; generally this means the right to receive dividends before such payment to ordinary shareholders. There could also be preference regarding the repayment of capital in the event of the company going into liquidation.

Preference shares that did not convert at some specific future date into ordinary shares used to be a common feature of the Australian financial scene, and they were traded freely on the sharemarket. These shares carried a fixed dividend which, unlike ordinary shares, was not adjusted upward to permit a share in any greater prosperity that the company might enjoy. This class of share was designed as a safe investment yielding a fixed income without the risks of ordinary shares. It was thus aimed at a different type of investor than one who would take up ordinary shares. But, with the increasing prosperity enjoyed by companies, the inability of these shares to participate in upward adjustments caused by inflation became a major limiting factor,[1] and they have

---

1. The Participating Preference Share was introduced in answer to this problem.

now virtually disappeared from the share trading scene, although many companies still possess them.

An investor should not normally take up shares of this nature, as they do not generally have any advantages over fixed-term securities, which have a maturity date and are secured. In the latter years of their trading on the sharemarket, preference shares were selling at discounts well below their par value to bring their yield into line with what could be expected from fixed-term securities. It was usual to issue different classes of preference shares (e.g. 'a' 'b' 'c') each with possibly a different dividend to accord with market conditions ruling at the time of issue.

Convertible Specified Preference Shares (new style)

Since the late 1970s a few companies have issued shares of this nature. These must be carefully distinguished from the old-fashioned preference shares referred to above. The predominant feature is that at some predetermined future date they will either be redeemed by the company for cash or they will be converted by the company into ordinary shares or into some other form of security. Shares of this nature are basically designed not so much for shareholder convenience but to fit the financial requirements of the company. In some circumstances the company may be able to pay the dividend on convertible shares from revenue and treat it as a charge against profits, thus obtaining a tax benefit. By comparison the dividend on ordinary shares must be paid from net profits and is not permitted as a tax-deductible item in arriving at the net profit of the company.

Other forms of convertible securities are also available. The main one is the convertible note. These are in fact debentures, which may or may not be secured, and which subsequently convert into ordinary shares at the discretion of the holder. Alternatively, the holder can elect to sell his notes on the market or redeem them for cash. A list of these notes with conversion factors and interest rates is available in the *Australian Stock Exchange Journal.*

Deferred Dividend Shares

Companies will pay 'dividends' on the shares that they issue. This is a payment to shareholders and is usually expressed in terms of 'cents per share'. A company must pay dividends out of realized net profits. A dividend paid upon ordinary shares is an appropriation of profits and can thus occur only if the company has made profits. Indeed, quite frequently ordinary shareholders will have to forgo their dividend when the company has made no profit or inadequate profit. On the other hand, the directors may, as a matter of financial policy, deliberately recommend that no dividend be paid even when profits have been earned, thus looking to the long-term financial viability of the company. New companies seeking to establish themselves financially will frequently adopt such a policy. Sometimes a type of share known as a deferred dividend share may be issued to recognize formally the nature of this type of project. Generally, however, a company will adjust its dividend on ordinary shares in line with the profit that it earns. Therefore, the return to the shareholder will, to some extent, keep pace with inflation.

In the case of preference shares the dividend will normally be specified, that is, prescribed at a set figure, which will be paid throughout the term of the shares (profits permitting). It will be preferential in the sense that it will be paid before any dividend is paid to ordinary shareholders. It may be cumulative in that if it cannot be paid in any particular year because of inadequate profits it will accumulate and remain owing to the shareholder in subsequent years when profits are sufficient to allow it to be paid out.

A company will sometimes pay a 'bonus dividend'. This is merely a gift dividend to shareholders over and above that which they could normally expect to receive. A company will sometimes pay such a dividend to mark its centenary or fifty years of business. A bonus dividend must be clearly distinguished from a bonus issue of shares, which is discussed later.

Timing of Dividend Payments

Normally dividends are paid twice a year. An interim dividend will be paid in respect of a particular year, usually during the currency of that year. A final dividend will then be paid after the company has had an opportunity to assess its profit for that particular year.

Dividend Amount

The amount of ordinary dividend a company may pay out is limited by at least three factors. First, the amount of profit earned. A company may not pay out an amount in dividends over and above its yearly profits. Second, the amount of dividend payout is limited by the availability of cash. In this respect, if a company has profits of $10,000 and cash of only $5000, it is limited to a payout amount of $5000. Thirdly, a dividend payout amount is limited by the policy directives of company directors. Often in the hope of maintaining the profitability of a company or expanding its operations, directors will retain some of the profits, which might otherwise be distributed in dividends.

The Dividend Yield on Shares

In respect of shares the dividend payout ratio of a company seldom accords with what is referred to as a dividend yield. This occurs because a payout ratio is calculated on the par or nominal value of the shares, whereas the yield is calculated on the shares' market value. An example will clear up any confusion.

Ampol shares have a nominal value of 50 cents in the dollar, so that if the company pays a 12½ cent dividend on every share, its dividend payout ratio is 25 per cent, i.e. 12½/50.

Although the nominal value of Ampol's shares is 50 cents, investors cannot buy them for this amount. They must buy them at their market value, which reflects the profitability and financial strength of Ampol and may be expected to be well above 50 cents. Assuming that Ampol's market value was $1 per share, this would make the dividend yield 12½ per cent (12½/1.00), considerably less than the dividend payout ratio.

As a rule, therefore, investors preferring high-yielding investments should invest in fixed-term securities, which are normally purchased at face value. On the other hand, if yield is considered secondary to capital gains, shares will be the better investment.

Conversely, if by some chance the investor obtains the shares at a figure much lower than their par value, the dividend yield will be much higher than the actual percentage dividend paid by the company.

By way of example, if the Ampol shares that have a nominal value of 50 cents are purchased by the investor at 25 cents rather than 50 cents and the company pays a 12½ cent dividend on every share, the yield will be 50 per cent, rather than 25 per cent when the share was selling for 50 cents.

This matter is further examined in chapter 7, 'Investment Decisions on the Sharemarket'.

Chapter Three
The Issue of Shares

Any public company has an unlimited right to issue shares provided it adheres to the provisions of the Companies Act and to the provisions set out in its own memorandum and articles of association. Usually a special resolution of the company will be required to issue shares.

Prospectus

Before approaching the public with an issue of shares, the company must issue a prospectus, a copy of which must be filed with the respective State Corporate Affairs Commission. The prospectus is a document (it is usually issued in the form of a booklet of A4 size) designed to give the potential investor as much information as practicable, not only the details of the particular share issue, but also relating to the broader financial position of the company. The Companies Act contains a quite extensive schedule of information that must be included in the prospectus. The failure of any company to provide this information will result in that company committing a legal offence. The prospectus will also usually contain the application form for investor purchase of shares. Applications will not normally be accepted unless this form is used. A prospectus may be issued through a broker, in which case the broker's stamp will appear in the top right-hand corner of the application form.

Before making any application for shares, the investor should read through the prospectus in full and make sure that he is conversant with the material and especially the terms and conditions. The prospectus constitutes the terms of a contract between the shareholder and the company, and the former cannot, after having accepted the shares, object to the terms and demand that the company take back the shares and refund his money. The only remedy available to the shareholders in such circumstances would be to sell the shares on the market, an action that might involve a financial loss.

Rarely, these days, will a company approach the public directly regarding a new issue of shares. An established company will almost invariably make a 'rights issue' of new shares to its existing shareholders. Thus, it is generally only a new company, or a company that is seeking access to the Australian market, or a company that is 'going public' after having been established for some years as a private company that will make a public issue. Frequently, shares will be placed privately, perhaps in payment for another business that the company is taking over, or to secure some other business benefit for the company. There is an increasing tendency for some companies to reserve considerable portions of new share issues for subscription by their own staff members. Tactics of this nature may appear unfair to members of the public who want to buy into a company that floats a new issue, but they are generally regarded as quite legitimate when viewed in the light of the financial or business requirements of the company.

Even if a company does issue directly to the public, it will often allocate the issue to accredited brokers who will in turn allocate the new issue to their own clients in a proportion of their own choosing. There have been occasions when the company has distributed the issue to a relatively limited number of larger brokers. This practice has been the subject of some controversy, as it means that unless an investor is a client of a big broker he will stand no chance of obtaining shares in a new issue. The counter argument is that practices of this nature tend to keep the issue of new shares on a rational basis. Allocating to accredited brokers enables them to maintain a relationship with clients who may have dealt with them for years and taken the bad times along with the good. Why should outsiders, who may have no other motive than quick speculation, be permitted to come in on a 'blue chip' new issue to the exclusion of investors who have had a steady relationship with the broker for years?

Generally, however, a company will seek to spread its shareholding as widely as possible to give the general public an interest in its activities. Usually the majority of shareholders hold parcels of under one thousand shares.

Investing in a New Issue of Shares

An application for shares has to be accompanied by the application money, and in some cases this will be the full amount payable on the shares. In other cases a further amount or possibly more than one further amount will be payable at a later date. These subsequent payments are referred to as 'calls' on the shares, but even if calls are payable the company will generally give the investor the option of paying the full amount owing on the shares in one instalment on application.

Having obtained all the applications, the company will, if there is an over-subscription, scale down the applications on a pro rata basis. The company has the option to refuse any applications. This will mean that it will probably have to make refunds to those persons who have not been allotted all the shares they applied for. A company may scale down the applications for a greater number of shares to a lesser extent than it scales down applications for small numbers to avoid administrative problems involved in handling very small parcels.

Allotment

Each successful shareholder will then be sent a letter of allotment setting out the number of shares that he has been allotted.

When the full amount has been paid on the shares, that is, where there are no calls owing, the company will issue a share certificate relating to the particular parcel of shares to individual shareholders. This will enable the shareholder to deal in the shares on the market. But companies will normally allow dealing in the shares on the basis of a letter of allotment. Thus a formal letter of allotment is a valuable document and should be treated as such by the shareholder.

Calls

If there are unpaid calls on the shares, the company has a right of lien on them, which means that the shareholder could forfeit the shares if the calls are not paid by the due date. The company will send out notices when calls are due. It is well to ensure that all shares purchased are fully paid up or at the least know what amount of equity you are buying. The investor who buys shares on the market on which calls can still be made may be required to pay the call to the company when it becomes due.

The Premium on Shares

Where a company has traded profitably for some time, it will generally issue new shares at above their par value. This is referred to as the issue of shares at a premium; the premium being the amount over and above the par value of the shares.

In the case of shares that have never been traded on the market before, the company will set the amount of the premium at its discretion. It can set it at whatever figure it chooses, but it will not, of course, set it at such a level as to discourage potential investors. Where the company already has shares trading on the market, the amount of the premium will be influenced by the current price of the company's shares on the stock exchange.

The company could not, of course, make a new issue dearer than its existing shares, as in such an event it would have no takers for the new issue. So there will usually be an appreciable margin between the take-up price of the new issue as against the existing price of the same company shares on the market.

The premium does not form part of the share capital of the company, but must be paid into a special reserve, often referred to as a 'share premium reserve'. There are restrictions on how the funds in this account can be used. The Companies Act specifies five such uses. Perhaps the most common uses are to facilitate the issuing of fully paid bonus shares and/or the paying up of unpaid amounts on members' shares.

Once the purchase or transfer of shares to an investor has been accepted by the company, the investor will be a member of the company and his name will be recorded in the share register that every company must keep.

Rights Issue of Shares

An established company that has been in business and trading profitably for some time, and whose shares are being quoted on the market, will not normally approach the general public when it wants to increase its capital and issue new shares. Instead it will make a 'rights issue' of the new shares by offering them to existing shareholders. Each existing shareholder will be offered the new shares in the proportion of his existing shareholding, be it one to five, one to ten, or so on, depending on the number of new shares the company wants to issue.

When making a rights issue the company will generally follow the same procedure as it would when issuing to the public. It will issue a prospectus that contains an application form and a prescribed date on or before which the applications must be lodged with the company.

Renounceable Rights Issue

Normally a rights issue will be renounceable, which means that the shareholder can sell his rights to the new issue on the market. This must be done through a broker in the same way as shares are sold. It is for this reason that an application form for rights is a valuable document, for a shareholder cannot sell his entitlement to the new shares without it. The document must be surrendered to the broker when the rights are sold.

The making of a rights issue as opposed to approaching the general public has the advantage of cutting down the company's administrative work. It also assists in maintaining a good relationship between the company and long-term shareholders.

Non-renounceable Rights Issue

In contrast to the above, a company may decide to make a non-renounceable issue, which means that the shareholder does not have the right to trade in his entitlement. It is common practice for small mining companies to issue shares on this basis, usually with the right to a minimum entitlement of one hundred shares.

This practice has been criticized by some shareholders, who argue that if they are unable to sell their rights and have not the cash to enable them to take up their entitlement, their existing shareholding has diminished in value in terms of its asset backing. That is, their existing holding represents a smaller share of the total assets of the company than it did prior to the new issue. This could well be the case, but on the other hand it can be argued from the company's point of view that a non-renounceable issue saves administrative time and expense, in that many small transfers of rights do not require to be registered. Also, the company can keep a much greater control over the persons who become shareholders when the issue is non-renounceable. Moreover, if the issue is non-renounceable, the company is not making a public issue and is not therefore required to issue a prospectus. This type of issue is also referred to as an entitlement issue.

Bonus Issues of Shares

A company that has enjoyed profitable trading for some years will frequently reward its shareholders with a 'bonus issue of shares'. This is simply an issue of shares to existing shareholders free of any payment by them. The bonus issue will, like a rights issue, be made in proportion to the existing shareholding. A bonus issue of one share for every two shares held would be an extremely generous issue. Normally, however, a bonus issue is in the ratio of one for five or one for ten.

Although the concept of free shares is very appealing to shareholders, it is worth pointing out that bonus shares are not as much of a gift as they seem. This is because, unlike a rights issue, no new equity is created by their issuance. Consider the following example. A shareholder with five shares is given a bonus issue of one for five. This means he gets one free share to take his total shareholding to six. Because no new equity is created, all that happens is that the shares previously held diminish in value. If five shares are worth $10, i.e. $2 each, six shares will be worth $1.66 each, because the total equity of $10 does not change.

What then are the advantages of a bonus issue? It is difficult to answer this question. It is often said that a bonus share is advantageous as long as dividends are maintained on the new share. However, this begs the question, why not just increase the dividend on the existing shares? This would save all the trouble of dealing with new shares. Listed below are one or two possible reasons.

(1) It disguises large increases in profit which, assuming this was to be passed on to shareholders, would otherwise show in increased dividends. This may have industrial relations consequences.
(2) It keeps the market price of the shares down, thus making them less costly to purchase and, given the

knowledge of their previous higher price, potentially profitable to subsequent investors.

(3) It may have a positive psychological effect upon investors assessing the financial strength of the company.

While for many companies it may be reasonable to assume that a bonus issue presupposes some growth in profit, the reverse assumption need not hold, nor indeed might it be the only reason for a bonus issue.

In respect of the former, there are those companies which, as a matter of financial policy, do not make bonus issues, even where these would appear appropriate in view of their financial position. In respect of the latter qualification, some companies have adopted a policy of small annual issues of bonus shares irrespective of growth in profitability. This strategy has been adopted in order to help maintain the image of the company in the market. Notwithstanding these qualifications it is the authors' experience that over the last few years the largest bonus issues have tended to be made by small, highly successful companies.

While bonus shares are designed to be in all respects similar to other ordinary shares in the company, this effect is not always immediate. Frequently bonus shares will carry a slight dividend differential for a short period of time. In practical terms this means that they may not qualify for the dividend due immediately following their issue. While the shares are in this state, they are generally referred to as 'new' and will generally sell on the market at a price marginally lower than the existing shares to allow for the differential in dividends.

Chapter Four
The Issue of Debenture Stock

A company will issue debenture stock (sometimes called fixed-term securities) in much the same manner as shares. Debentures differ from shares, however, in two basic ways. Firstly, they do not form part of the company's capital, and, secondly, they must be bought back by the company.

Once a company decides that its financial position necessitates the borrowing of term finance and it passes the necessary resolution, it will issue a prospectus inviting the public to invest. The prospectus calling for debenture finance will contain an application form, which the investor must detach and submit to the company by the prescribed date. Applications in any other form will not be accepted. Investors who place funds in this form of investment usually trade-off capital gains for higher yields.

Application

The full amount that the investor proposes to invest must usually be sent in with the application. Companies will not usually be burdened with over-subscriptions in respect of debenture finance because when the amount they require is obtained they will declare the issue closed. Sometimes they will accept over-subscriptions.

Companies may not issue debentures at a premium, but there have been a very few occasions when it was difficult to obtain debenture finance, when such finance was issued at a discount. This meant that at maturity the investor was repaid more than was originally invested. Such a practice is, of course, highly unusual, and will be adopted only in circumstances when the company is desperate for finance.

The return on debenture stock is at a specified rate of interest. It does not vary in the nature of a dividend. The specified rate of interest is owing to the investor throughout the life of the security and, except in the unlikely event of renegotiation of the contract, will not be varied either upwards or downwards during the term of the loan.

Debenture Security

The expression 'debenture' means, in effect, a written acknowledgement of a debt. Although in some cases this written acknowledgement of indebtedness by a company may be deemed to be sufficient security, in most cases additional security in the form of a floating charge over assets will be offered. This charge will crystallize in the event of default of payment of either interest or principal by the company. In the event of such a situation occurring, a trustee will usually act on behalf of debenture holders. This trustee is required to be appointed by the company at the outset of its debenture issue. Details of this are set out in the prospectus announcing the debenture issue.

The charge granted to debentures will usually be a first charge over the assets of the company, which means that should the company default the debenture-holders will take priority over other creditors.

Comparison of Shareholders and Debenture-holders in Relation to the Company

1. *Rights of Membership*
It is well to bear in mind the distinction between shareholders and debenture-holders in respect of their relationship to the company.

The shareholder is a member of the company, with the right to receive notices of and vote at meetings. He may take part in a democratic manner in the running of the company. He may speak at meetings and put forward motions. Admittedly, in practice this is not the case, because most companies are firmly under the political control of the directors. However, machinery exists in the Companies Act for the protection of minority shareholders in cases where the conduct of the majority is improper or detrimental to the interests of the minority.

Once the company has arrived at a validly executed decision, the shareholder is expected to abide by that decision. Should he not like what the company is doing, his immediate remedy is to sell his shareholding and cease to be a member of that company. The rights of the shareholder are enforced through the articles and memorandum, and if any contract exists between the shareholder and the company, it is very vague.

The debenture-holder, on the other hand, is not a member of the company. He has no right to vote at general company meetings. He will have a vote in respect of the affairs of the company only if there is a default in respect of his claims and the receiver or manager calls a meeting of creditors. This, of course, is rare. The debenture-holder is a creditor of the company and is subject to the terms of the contract that he has concluded with the company when he originally invested. The terms of this contract will be set out in the prospectus from which the application form will have been detached. The submission of the application form, together with the cheque, amounts to an offer by the investor to accept the terms of the contract set out in the prospectus. When the company accepts the application, the contract is concluded, and both parties are thereby bound. The terms of this contract can be altered only by renegotiation between the parties. Once the amount of the loan is repaid, the contract between the company and the debenture-holder is at an end.

2. *Investment Return*
In view of the fact that participation in the running of

a company may not be an effective point of difference between the shareholder and debenture-holder, interest immediately turns to investment return.

Unlike the shareholder, the debenture-holder is entitled to a fixed rate of interest, which is specified in the initial contract. Beyond this, however, he will not normally participate in the extra profits of the company in the form of dividends and bonus share issues. Conversely, however, the debenture-holder does not have to suffer from downturns in profitability as ordinary shareholders do. In the latter case the rights of the debenture-holder are similar to those of the preference shareholder, which poses the question: What is the difference between the two investment opportunities? The answer is that the debenture-holder has priority over the preference shareholder when capital is returned in the event of liquidation. The preference shareholder, in turn, has priority over the ordinary shareholder.

Other Debenture-issuing Bodies

Although we have concentrated on debenture or fixed-term security issues by companies, other bodies can also issue this type of investment. For example, both the federal government and state government authorities (e.g. the state electricity bodies) may issue fixed-term securities. In fact, in terms of the volume of this security traded, semi-government issues far exceed company issues, and are second only to ordinary shares across the entire market. More on these securities later.

Chapter Five
Share and Debenture Certificates

Share Certificates

Having purchased shares and been registered as a member of a company, a shareholder will be issued with a share certificate. This will show the actual number and class of shares that are registered in the holder's name as well as routine details of the company.

The share certificate is not a negotiable instrument. As such, title to the shares cannot be transferred merely by passing the certificate to another person. The act of registration with the company is the means of transferring shares. Many years ago some local authorities did issue debenture certificates that were negotiable, but these have long since disappeared. Even so, shareholders should ensure that they retain their certificates in a safe place — for example, in safe custody in a bank.

It is not possible to deal in shares without the physical possession of the certificate, which must be surrendered to the company when any dealing in the shares takes place. If a share certificate is lost, application can be made to the company for a duplicate, but the company will normally require that the shareholder supply a letter indemnifying it in the event of any loss that it may suffer as the result of issuing the new certificate. The exact procedure may, however, vary greatly between different companies. Some require a statutory declaration executed by the shareholder, while some go so far as to require the loss to be advertised in the Public Notice section of a newspaper.

Share Registrars

The registration of shareholders can be a very extensive administrative procedure, and this is especially so in the case of a large company whose shares are frequently traded. For this reason many companies now use the services of professional share registrars. These are usually insurance companies or banks who run a share registry division. All communication of a routine nature involving the shares should be made not to the company itself but to the registrar. However, a number of small companies still keep their own share registers.

Debenture Securities Certificates

Certificates are also issued in respect of debenture securities. They are very similar to share certificates. The major difference between debenture and share certificates is in respect of the information contained on the certificate. Both the rate of interest and the maturity date will appear on the debenture certificate. Because a share has no maturity date and (except for preference shares) no fixed rate of interest, these details will not appear on an ordinary share certificate.

A shareholder may have more than one certificate in any one company and it is thus necessary to ensure that the correct certificate is chosen when dealing in the various securities. This is especially so when a company has more than one maturity of specified preference shares, the certificates of which need to be submitted to the company for conversion at different dates.

Chapter Six
The Sharemarket, Investors, and Brokers

The Australian Stock Exchange

Share trading in Australia began towards the end of the last century. Currently the market is organized around six major exchanges, any one of which may be used to buy and sell shares. These exchanges are located in Adelaide, Brisbane, Hobart, Melbourne, Perth, and Sydney.[1] Although these exchanges operate in different parts of the country, it should be noted that there is only one Australia-wide market for shares. Accordingly an investor does not achieve any advantage by attempting to deal with any one exchange to the exclusion of others.

As an aid towards furthering uniformity of activity by stock exchanges, in 1937 the six major exchanges set up a company (limited by guarantee) known as the Australian Associated Stock Exchange (AASE). The aims of this body include the protection of the welfare of its members, the protection of the interests of members of the public, and the adoption of uniform rules and regulations pursuant to the above two aims. These rules and regulations are the 'stock exchange listing requirements'.

Listing on the Stock Exchange

Basically the 'listing requirements' specify the circumstances under which a company may have its shares

---

1. There are also unofficial stock exchanges in Ballarat, Bendigo, and Newcastle.

traded on the Australian exchanges. These rules are strict and provide a very effective code for maintaining standards of business conduct in Australia.

In brief, the conditions that must be fulfilled before listing are: the capital must be in excess of a certain figure, the shares must be freely negotiable, the company must maintain appropriate standards of business conduct, and it must supply the exchange with all information likely to affect trading in its shares. Among this information is included a set of financial statements produced in prescribed format and detailing prescribed information. Should these standards not be met in the judgement of the AASE, the company will not be registered in the first place or, should it be registered, it may be suspended from trading. As listing offers considerable advantage, particularly in respect of company access to public funds, companies try to comply with these rules. So the fact that a company is listed affords the public considerable protection as it amounts to a guarantee that certain minimum standards have been met.

An investor should thus be very careful in purchasing shares in a company that is not listed. This does not mean that such shares are automatically to be shunned, but great care should be taken to check the viability of the company and whether or not the shares can be sold should the holder want to dispose of them. There are some very good smaller companies trading in a highly profitable manner that are not listed, but if an investor is offered shares in an unlisted company, he would do well to ask himself the question, 'Why does the seller want to dispose of these shares?'

It is quite common for companies to trade for some time without seeking listing and then to find that their capacity for expansion is hampered without the attribute of their shares being quoted on the exchange. To reiterate an earlier point, having one's shares listed allows a company access to a market in which considerable amounts of funding are up for grabs. There has been a tendency for the number of companies listed to decline over recent years because of the takeovers and amalgamations that have taken place.

The Marketable Parcel and Odd Lots

Before shares can be traded on the exchange they must be in what is known as a marketable parcel. There are five such parcels. The number of shares in each parcel differs according to the nominal value of the share. They are as follows:

1 cent to 25 cents	— 2000 shares
26 cents to 50 cents	— 1000 shares
51 cents to $1	— 500 shares
$1.01 to $10	— 500 shares
$10.01 and over	— 50 shares

Although it is not possible to trade in anything other than marketable parcels, it can occur that investors can acquire shares in less than marketable lots. This can occur where a company makes either a bonus or rights issue of shares. When an investor holds shares that do not make up a parcel, this is referred to as an 'odd lot'.

In this situation the investor has two options open. Either he must seek to buy the number of shares he requires to make up a marketable parcel or he must sell the shares. In both cases this trading is done through specialized brokers who deal in 'odd lots'. It is worth noting that the price of these shares is usually a little lower than the normal price. This is to compensate the broker for his job of matching these 'odd lots' to others to form marketable parcels.

Trading on the Floor of the Exchange

Each stock exchange has a trading floor on which the share transactions take place. Attached to the walls will be the trading boards that contain the names of every listed company. Note that there are two boards — these are referred to as the high activity and low activity boards. The shares on the high activity board are of the leading companies, which trade most often, while the low activity board contains the names of companies that do not trade so frequently. The market leaders appear on the high activity board.

Trading takes place at a morning session and an afternoon session at 10 a.m. and 2.30 p.m., respectively. Each firm of brokers has its operator's post on the floor of the exchange where buying and selling instructions can be received direct from the operator's firm. The Sydney Stock Exchange presently has forty-two member firms, and each firm is identified in the market by an operating number.

Buying and selling quotes are posted on the boards. At the beginning of each trading session bids made by buyers and offers by sellers are recorded. The board on the trading floor is usually divided into 8 sections as follows:

(i)	(ii)	(iii)	(iv)	(v)	(vi)	(vii)	(viii)
XYZ	97	123	125	66	126	128 125	125

where (i) is the abbreviated name of the company
    (ii) is the buying broker's number
    (iii) is the bid in cents
    (iv) is the offer in cents
    (v) is the selling broker's number
    (vi) is the first sale of the day
    (vii) is the high and low for the day
    (viii) is the last sale of the day.

If there is agreement between a buyer and seller so that a sale is made, this will be recorded by the 'chalkie', who, on the advice of the selling sharebroker, will remove the sharebroker's number and bid from the board.

The sales turnover for the day (including the top ten) and closing quotes for all companies are compiled on a continuous basis and made available to the public by the exchange twice daily, generally within two hours of the closing of each session.

Profile of Investors

The sharemarket today accommodates a very wide

variety of investors. The days when it was limited to investment by institutions, with a few businessmen and elderly widows, have long since gone. All kinds of Australians now invest on the sharemarket, from teenagers to large insurance companies. But one or two patterns are still evident in the different categories of investors. As expected, the large institutions tend to purchase the largest parcels of shares. Elderly persons tend to be the least active: they will purchase shares and hold them for many years without dealing in them. Businessmen tend to be the most active dealers but, on the other hand, farmers seem to be somewhat languid investors, tending to plough back any liquid funds into their own properties.

There is no mystique about investing on the sharemarket. It is possible for any person, with a minimum of effort, to acquire sufficient knowledge to deal successfully in shares.

Sharebrokers and Their Activities

A private individual cannot directly make use of a stock exchange. He must act through an accredited broker, that is, a person who is authorized by the particular stock exchange to transact business, and is thus a member of the exchange. In accordance with the Securities Code (1982) no person may act as a sharebroker unless licensed to do so by the National Companies and Securities Commission.

Sharebrokers are entitled to hold shares in their own name. However, when dealing as a principal they are not permitted to purchase any securities. Most firms of brokers do not confine their activities to the buying and selling of shares on behalf of clients, but carry on such duties as acting as underwriters or agents for the government or local authorities when they approach the public for finance. You will find that brokers' offices are literally inundated with prospectuses of all kinds. Brokers are paid a brokerage fee in respect of the transactions they carry out on behalf of investors. (See Appendix A.)

Some of the larger firms employ research staff whose job it is to gather and interpret financial data relevant to the sharemarket and to individual companies. This information will frequently be made available to the brokers' clients in the form of a newsletter. Brokers give advice to clients regarding possible purchases. This matter is considered in more detail in succeeding chapters.

The Transfer of Shares

As already stated, if an investor wants to sell or purchase shares on the sharemarket, he must operate through a broker. Having received an order, the broker will relay it to his operator, possibly by phone or telex. If a sale is made, the broker will then draw up a 'contract note', which is sent to the client. This shows details of the transaction, including the number of shares bought or sold, the brokerage, and usually the date on which settlement is required together with the amount by which the client's account has been debited or credited. Normally all share purchases are due for settlement on receipt of the contract note.

The selling broker will then draw up a share transfer, which must be on the prescribed form. This will be submitted to the seller for his signature. It is not necessary that the transfer be signed by the buyer. This form, together with the share certificate of the seller, must then be submitted to the company, which will erase the name of the seller of the shares from the register of members and insert that of the buyer or, if not all of the shareholding of the seller has been disposed of, make the appropriate amendment to the number of shares that he holds. The company will then send a certificate to the purchaser of the shares. At one time investors used to experience considerable delays in obtaining certificates from companies, but with the increased use of share registry firms this has now been substantially eliminated. The signatures on share transfer forms do not need to be witnessed, but the investor must show his address and the place where the form is signed.

Transactions in respect of other forms of stock are made in much the same manner. As the holders of local authority and government stock are registered with the Reserve Bank, transfers in that category of stock must be submitted to the bank for registration.

Chapter Seven
Investment Decisions on the Sharemarket

The Required Psychological Profile

An essential prerequisite for successful investing is to develop an appropriate mental attitude. Movements in the share price index are sometimes unpredictable and frequently quite irrational. This fact must be accepted by a potential investor. That there will be some losses must be accepted as inevitable. No one can expect to be a winner all the time, in any walk of life, let alone in the share investing business.

An investor should not be too concerned with losses on any one or a few parcels of shares, but should be concerned with his overall position. Losses on individual parcels of shares are, on occasions, absolutely unavoidable, and unless an investor can learn to live with these he is going to lead a miserable life. An oft-quoted maxim for the investor is that one should invest only the amount one can afford to lose.

One event that agitates many investors is to have sold shares and then to see them rise substantially in price. However, some people have made fortunes by selling shares at the wrong time and investing in an even more profitable enterprise.

It is well to avoid the get-rich-quick mentality. The Australian sharemarket is of such a size and nature that very substantial capital gains are only occasionally possible. Moreover, it usually takes the investment of very large amounts to obtain large capital gains. The investor is well advised to think in terms of obtaining small profits over a long period of time — a hundred dollars here, twenty or thirty dollars there, and ten dollars somewhere else.

Probably the best mental attitude for the small investor is to regard investing as an absorbing hobby, an interesting topic for conversation with those of like mind, of whom there is an increasing number.

Some people regard investing in the sharemarket as a form of gambling. However, while there is always an element of risk, this can be very much reduced by attention and experience. Experience is gained by daily study of general information pertaining to the sharemarket. This is not necessarily an onerous task, for the required information is available in daily newspapers, or stock exchange reports.

For those investors not disposed to spend time gathering information, nor indeed to weather the vagaries of the sharemarket, the alternatives are to invest in particular types of securities (requiring much less attention) or to place themselves in the hands of a good broker. But more on these matters later.

An investor has the option of selling his entire holding and remaining aloof from the market at any time. This advantage is not always available for those who purchase the assets of a business. However, selling his entire holding should be done only at a time when the investor will make a profit by the deal.

The selling of an entire portfolio may be desirable in cases where the investor is planning a lengthy absence from Australia, as it is difficult or at least inconvenient to obtain daily information on the Australian market when one is abroad. Communication with a broker may prove a problem as well as being costly.

Share Trading to Beat Inflation

It is frequently claimed that investing in company shares provides a hedge against inflation and is thus preferable to investment in fixed-term, and fixed-income securities. While this may be true for some shares, not all shares increase in price with the passage of time. Indeed, some have actually declined in value over the past five or so years and others have remained quite stationary. Thus an investor cannot purchase just any share and expect it automatically to provide him with a cover against decline in the value of money.

Further, paper profits are of little use. No investor is protecting himself against inflation if he simply sits on shares and sees them go up to a peak and then decline to a price well below what he paid for them. A profit must be in the pocket of the investor before it can be considered as such. Thus continued trading is usually essential to preserve one's portfolio against inflation. If the investor is not only to keep up with inflation, but also to keep ahead of it, constant trading is imperative.

There are two vital factors associated with trading in shares. These are selecting the correct shares and making sure of the correct timing of sales and purchases. Much of the remainder of this book is devoted to these two points. A firm grasp of these two principles is the hallmark of the competent investor.

Macro-economic Factors Affecting the Sharemarket

Macro-economic factors are those affecting the market as a whole (though not necessarily the whole market in the same way), rather than individual firms. Although since the late 1960s and early 1970s a considerable amount of research has been undertaken in an attempt to link general sharemarket reactions to various economic factors, debate rages on the conclusiveness of the various findings. Although this debate languishes in methodological questions, several factors seem inevitably to have an effect on the market, and therefore should be considered when making investment decisions.

One factor that we have already mentioned is inflation. Of all the factors this is probably the hardest to evaluate. This is because inflation is a many-faceted phenomenon. While it is possible for the general level of share prices to be rising, it is also possible for the shares of companies in some sectors to remain constant or even fall. One would thus expect rational investors wishing to hedge against inflation to move out of some shares into others, thus forcing change on the market. Accepting the inconstancy of shares in inflationary times, it is therefore advisable that investors engage in constant trading or, at the very least, constant re-evaluation to preserve their portfolios against financial erosion.

A second factor influencing the market is government policy. Besides changes in monetary policy that may affect inflation, the government may institute changes in fiscal policy resulting in changes to the tax structure. Such a case might occur where in an effort to encourage export, incentives in the form of tax rebates are offered to successful exporting companies. The result is that these companies will tend to reflect these incentives in their profits and represent comparatively better investment opportunities. The time to invest in these companies is before the incentives show up. Thus speculation about changes in government policy, which may cause some presently unprofitable company to prosper in the future, may be expected to bring about some movement in the market. Other government decisions that are likely to have an effect upon the market include price-control policies and monopoly-control policies. Price controls tend to depress profitability and growth, depressing the market, while companies that have a monopoly or near monopoly in a business field tend to be better investment targets. Consequently any policy affecting the position of a company within a business sector is likely to have an effect on the market. BHP, for example, has until recently had something of a monopoly in the steel industry. Recent decisions by the government not to curb steel imports have, however, forced the company to lay off staff in an effort to curb falling profitability and retain investor confidence.

A third factor likely to influence the market is the state of the world economy. Australia, because of its dependence on exports, is not immune to movements in the economic climate of trading partners, particularly the United States of America. For example, a recent rally on the American sharemarket led to a similar recovery in Australia.

A fourth factor likely to affect the general market for shares is the state of other investments. Anything in the outside economy that serves to attract funds away from the sharemarket will usually reduce the demand for shares, and therefore prices will decline. One such alternate investment prospect is the property market. Should property become attractive, it will attract funds away from the sharemarket, and vice versa.

A fifth factor that may have an influence on the market is cash injection. It is clear that there must be some initial infusion of cash into the sharemarket to bring an upsurge in prices. This cash will generally come, initially, from outside the market. The greater the flow of cash into the sharemarket, the greater will tend to be the demand for shares, causing an upward pressure on the prices. This in turn could attract still more cash into the sharemarket as the rising share prices will increase the expectations of still greater capital gains. Once a market rise has been initiated, it can accelerate by feeding off its own innate dynamism. Thus the expectation of profit will cause investors to continue to sell some shares and to reinvest in other shares. Provided that sharemarket reinvestment is encouraged and the funds do not go elsewhere, there will be a high level of demand and prices will tend to rise.

A sixth factor likely to influence the market in a general way is the issue of new stock. Heavy demands for company capital in the form of initial flotations of shares could, for example, dampen the demand for existing shares on the market. Correspondingly a large number of rights issues or even large numbers of bonus issues can also cause prices to decline, by easing the demand for shares. On the other hand, the issue of debenture stock does not appear to affect the sharemarket to the same extent, as it does not offer the possibility of a capital gain.

One other factor should be mentioned. It has been said that the sharemarket will tend to be at a high level in an election year because it will serve the incumbent government to maintain the appearance of prosperity. This contention has still to be sustained. It is true that the expectation of the election of a government manifestly hostile to business may cause a downturn in the market, but this does not seem likely in Australia.

For those who may be frustrated by the lack of specific direction in respect of how macro-economic factors affect the sharemarket, it should be pointed out that it has not yet been possible to quantify accurately the specific effect of any of the factors mentioned, let alone a series of these factors operating concurrently. However, it is worth noting that investors have worked and prospered under these conditions since securities were first traded.

Economic Forces Influencing Sectors of the Market or Individual Companies

We have looked at some of the variables that may affect the overall level of the sharemarket, but there is no guarantee that any individual company will move in accordance with the general trend of the market. Frequently, economic forces will affect particular segments of industry or even individual companies without having a general influence on the sharemarket as a whole. Investors should be aware of such problems because they are far more likely to influence the price of individual shares than broader economic trends. Some of these will now be looked at.

One of the prerequisites for sound share prices is for a company to have a consistently good profit record. Broadly speaking, the companies with the best performance are those with above-average profit records. Even on a rising market it will generally be found that companies with very poor profit performance do not rise as fast as others or, indeed, may not rise at all. Techniques for measuring company profit rates will be considered elsewhere, but presently we are concerned with factors likely to affect sectors of companies or individual companies. Some knowledge of these matters is essential to the prudent investor.

Frequently, sectors of industry will be depressed when other sectors are thriving, or some companies can make a profit when others are finding it hard to survive. Many of the factors mentioned as macro factors above also have a micro effect, that is, may affect individual firms and sectors. In respect of individual company profitability, government policy is likely, in instances where tax and other incentives are given to encourage certain business operations, to favour some firms over others. Other factors likely to affect an individual company's standing in the market include company management and company diversification.

1. *Company Management*
Management can be a vital force in profitability. In some cases even one individual can dramatically alter the financial position of a company. If a company has been built up to a position of high prosperity by one individual, it is possible that the loss of that person could have a drastic effect on its profit levels.

In general, the management of Australian companies is, by world standards, quite efficient. However, there are a number of old-established companies that have stodgy and quite conservative management policies, and as a growth prospect such companies are not exciting. Such companies, if they are to be worth investing in, must have other attributes, such as valuable assets.

2. *Company Diversification*
A firm is said to be diversified if its profit is earned not from one but from a number of distinct business activities. In practical terms this means that a firm primarily involved in the building industry may acquire interests in the manufacturing industry, primary industry, and the investment industry. It diversifies because some industries are more resistant to economic downturn than others. The building industry, for example, has been recognized as sensitive to economic fluctuations. Thus if there is a downturn in the economy, firms solely engaged in the building industry, as well as their suppliers, can be in trouble. A highly diversified company will weather economic vagaries better than a one-product company. Consequently there has been a tendency in recent years

for Australian companies, especially the larger ones, to diversify. This is not to say that one-product companies should be avoided. It could well be that a boom in that one product will result in substantial growth in the short term, for the company's full resources can be devoted to that one product. Notwithstanding this qualification, a diversified company will tend to fare better in the long run.

General

The factors described above do not represent a complete schedule of the economic influences likely to affect share prices. Specific circumstances affecting particular shares must always be taken into consideration, and these can be learned only by constantly keeping one's ear to the ground.

Let's look at some other points to be considered when choosing shares.

Chapter Eight
Selecting Shares

Market Leaders

A few companies stand out in almost every respect — size, profitability, marketability of shares — these companies are generally referred to as 'market leaders'. Trends in the market are usually reflected initially in the shares of these companies, and fluctuations in their shares will tend to carry the rest of the market with them.

This is not to say that an investor should purchase shares in this class to the exclusion of all others. Some of the best growth has taken place in recent years in shares of smaller companies. Some market leaders are slow movers, both in an upward and downward direction. For this reason a decision to invest in a market leader rather than other shares must be based on an assessment of the extent to which an investor is willing to substitute a steady dividend income for possible capital gains. It is generally accepted that while market leaders afford a steady and reasonable dividend income, they do not constitute shares on which significant capital gains can regularly be made. Consequently a security-conscious investor will prefer the market leader with its steady dividend of income to non-market leaders in which to some extent a trade-off must be made between steady dividend income and possible capital gains.

A point worth noting is that shares classified as market leaders change with time. Some market leaders will lose their status and be replaced by others. In general, shares that change hands on a daily basis in moderate volume, can reasonably be regarded as market leaders.

Choosing Shares

When making a choice between the shares of individual companies, a factor of vital importance is the potential for growth of a particular company and its shares. The question then becomes: how does one assess growth and the potential for growth? In the previous chapter we considered broad economic forces that were likely to have an effect on growth. Our qualifying conclusion from this discussion was that while these factors affected growth, few tangible (and proven) models were available to assess the effect of these factors on individual companies. In the absence of these models one is forced to look for evidence of company growth, e.g. productivity, profitability.

Perhaps the most easily assessable of these is company profitability. One quite simple way of assessing growth is to look at a series of reported profit figures of a company and see in what direction they have moved, upwards or downwards. A steady increase in profitability and/or productivity can be used as simple measures of growth. Notwithstanding the fact that high productivity and profit will generally be essential preconditions for company growth, growth by itself is meaningless to an investor, unless that growth manifests itself in some tangible way to the benefit of the investor. The following represent ways in which growth is of value to the shareholder:

Share Price
Firstly, there should be a continued rise in the price of the share over a period. There can be minor downturns, but the long-term trend must be upward, especially in relation to any upward trend in the market as a whole.

Bonus Issues
Secondly, growth can show itself in frequent bonus

issues. These, of course, are very desirable to the individual shareholder, who can either sell the bonus shares when he receives them or retain them and thereby increase the yield on the parcel of those shares held, which has the effect of diminishing the capital cost of the parcel as a whole. The implications of the bonus issue will be discussed more fully shortly. A few Australian companies have adopted the policy of frequent bonus issues — some in fact have annual bonuses, and these shares are usually keenly priced.

Rights Issues
Thirdly, growth can be observed in frequent rights issues to existing shareholders. When a company finds that it needs more capital to finance its infrastructure, it will make a new issue of shares, usually to existing holders. There will always be a bonus element of some magnitude in a rights issue. More of this later.

Dividends
Fourthly, growth can be reflected in progressively increasing dividend payments. A company will usually increase its dividend when it is prospering. In some cases bonus dividends may also be paid.

A good record in these matters will usually force up the price of a company's shares. The astute investor will look for a share that is low priced, but which has the prospect of growth in the future. This will generally cause the price of shares to rise, increasing the possibility of capital gains. Of course this requires the ability to forecast the likely future profitability of the company and to gauge the likelihood of economic growth in the field in which the company operates. In the absence of such an ability, investors should seek the advice of those who have made a specialty of acquiring such knowledge, that is, brokers.

Marketability
If a share does not trade regularly on the market, then it is very difficult for growth to occur. The marketability

of a particular share is vitally important in determining whether or not it is a suitable purchase. It is here that the market leader comes into its own. But the issue of marketability requires further consideration.

There are some shares, mainly in smaller companies, which do not frequently trade. This infrequency can be due to a number of possible reasons. There could, of course, be no demand for the shares, but this is a rare occurrence. The shares may be very closely held, with little inclination on the part of the current holders to sell them. The company may be so small with so few shares that there are simply insufficient shares to meet demand. On the Australian sharemarket, there is a reasonable number of small but highly profitable companies that fall within these latter two categories.

So the fact that a share does not frequently trade does not automatically exclude it from being a good buy. The investor should assess the worth of the company before holding back on the grounds of lack of marketability. In a time of market depression, shares in companies of this nature may come onto the market at bargain prices and the astute investor should be on the lookout for them. It may be that a family trust or estate has been forced to sell its holding in such a company. Having purchased such shares, the investor may decide to hold them because of their growth potential, rather than attempt to make a quick capital gain by selling them shortly after purchase. This would be a matter for consideration on the individual merit of each share.

Security
It is usually unwise to purchase shares in a company that does not appear to be financially sound. But, here again, some degree of qualification is required.

Financial Soundness
The inexperienced investor should purchase shares only in companies that are financially sound. Here again the market leader comes to the fore, as market leaders are rarely in financial difficulties.

However, this is not to say that shares in a company

that is not presently in the top bracket financially cannot be a good investment. The key question is, what are the future growth prospects of that company? A share that could well be a good buy would be one in a company that has a long-term record of financial strength, but which is having temporary difficulties. In this event, the share may be artificially underpriced. However, such situations require the ability to assess financial data relating to the company as well as being able to assess accurately future economic conditions in the industry concerned. As such, these investment opportunities are not for investment novices.

Shares in a company on the verge of bankruptcy may still trade and can also be quite a sound investment, depending on price. Technically, in the event of liquidation, shareholders are entitled to the assets after debtors have been paid in full. Should the assets exceed the total market value of the company the shareholders still, in theory at least, have a potentially valuable investment. But such a situation rarely occurs in practice, as the assets are usually long since disposed of, or there is a successful takeover bid, before the company reaches the point of liquidation.

Investment in a financially unsound company is therefore not to be avoided in all circumstances, but the novice investor would do well to confine his activities to companies with a proven track record.

The Portfolio
It is a well-established maxim of investors that one does not place all one's eggs in the same basket. Even a relatively small amount of investment money should be spread among different companies. The competent investor will establish a portfolio of shares — an array of shares from different companies, designed to yield a maximum of growth spread over a number of different sectors open to investment. It is advisable to have two or three market leaders in the portfolio. The rest could comprise shares in good growth potential companies, but not necessarily the most actively traded shares. This could include those chosen for their return in the form

of a large specific yield owing to the low price at which the shares were purchased.

The portfolio should not extend too widely, although it is difficult to lay down specific rules. Probably about a dozen companies would be desirable, as greater numbers tend substantially to increase the administrative problems. A novice investor should spread his risks. The experienced investor can use his experience to purchase larger parcels of a lesser number of shares.

A portfolio should be kept under constant review. If a share fails to live up to expectations, then remove it from your portfolio, and replace it with a better performer.

Chapter Nine
Share Purchase Strategy

Ups and Downs in the Market

The sharemarket is prone to rise and fall in cycles. As already stated, these trends in the market will, on the whole, usually be led by the market leaders, but may be evident in many second-line shares which react more sharply to market fluctuations. There will be some companies whose shares tend to 'stick' and will not move with the broader market trends.

The experienced investor must be able to determine the correct time to sell or buy. Until you have gained some familiarity with share price reaction to various market changes, it is advisable to maintain regular consultation with your investment broker. After a while you will begin to learn how various market factors are likely to affect your particular portfolio. Once you feel confident about your ability to judge the probable effect of a change in the market, all you need do is pay regular attention to the state of the market. At the simplest level this can be accomplished by reading the financial pages of newspapers.

Sometimes the market is clearly too high and must come down. At such times the prudent investor will not purchase shares, but may be tempted to sell. If it is clear that a long-term downswing in the market is about to take place, it could pay to unload an entire portfolio and place funds in fixed-income securities to at least hold the value of one's savings. When it is clear that the market has reached rock bottom and that a rise must soon take place, the investor can then remove his savings from fixed-income securities and recommence the purchase of shares at the lower prices. Nothing is to be gained by holding on to a mass of shares, or indeed any share, when the prices are tumbling. Any sentimental attachment to shares that inhibits them from being sold under any circumstances is not a healthy investment attitude.

Glamour Shares — the Underpriced and the Overpriced Share

In the past, some Australian shares have sold at a premium above their actual worth compared with other shares and/or the general state of the market. This condition is not so evident at the present time. Some shares have 'peaked' at high prices at particular times and subsequently fallen, never to regain the peak price. Often it is not easy to see precisely what creates this psychological affinity of the market to particular shares. In one case it was the evolution of a new transport technology that appeared to assume the magnitude of a revolution. In another case, it was the advent of a type of company not frequently seen on the market in former years.

The investor should be wary of shares that appear overpriced. If you happen to hold such shares, then you should consider selling them. On the other hand, shares are not normally undervalued for any length of time in this country, although it is quite a common occurrence on sharemarkets overseas. But shares can be underpriced in the short term. This can happen in the case of a company that has a very good financial record before the market catches up with such information, or where the market is momentarily flooded with shares due to a restructuring of the capital of a company. This oversupply will eventually be fully taken up by the market, thus returning the share to a more realistic price.

Long-term or Short-term Investing?

As already indicated, it is not usually advisable to hold on to shares falling in price. This raises the wider question of whether it is advisable to purchase shares with the intention of shortly selling them or of holding them for a substantial period, possibly a lifetime. Generally, short-term investing is to be preferred. If an investor sees the opportunity for a capital gain, it is advisable to get the profit into his pocket and then look around for some other opening for the funds.

In some cases long-term investing has a lot to commend it. If the market proves relatively stable over a substantial period, the yield (dividend/market price of share) on good growth shares may well exceed that on fixed-term securities, especially if the investor can get good secure shares at a low capital price with the prospect of bonus issues, which could increase the yield still further. Such shares could yield more than fixed-term securities and possibly even a capital gain once the market starts to move upwards.

However, it must be admitted that really good yields are normally possible only when market prices are very low. Thus it is always advisable for the investor to assess the possible yield from selling his parcel at the current prices and investing in government securities or even in debenture stock against the yield he is currently getting from his shares.

Throughout 1980 and in the early part of 1981, the market was not conducive to satisfying yields. So within that period, it was preferable to invest short-term for capital gain. Once again, your broker will be able to acquaint you with your options.

Purchasing and Taking Up Rights

When a company wishes to issue new capital, but for various reasons does not wish to offer the issue directly to the general public, it will make what is known as a rights issue in which existing shareholders are allocated first priority to the shares. In order to promote a new issue of shares to existing shareholders, the company will pitch the price of the rights to the existing shareholders at somewhat less than the current market price of the existing shares. A company whose shares are at a very low level, possibly below par even, would find it extremely difficult, if not impossible, to float a rights issue. However, if the shares are above par, the company will inevitably attempt to issue at a premium. Should the shares be rising on the market, the 'bonus' will be progressively more attractive with the rise of the existing shares.

In deciding whether to take up the rights to the new issue or to sell his entitlement, the investor should always examine the market situation. If the entitlement is small, and it is not possible for the investor to make a marketable parcel out of the rights together with his existing holding, it will probably be advisable to dispose of them. Similarly, should he already have a substantial holding in the company and feel that the price of those particular shares may fall in the near future, it again may be desirable to sell the entitlement.

The presence of a rights issue trading on the market will normally have the effect of depressing the price of the existing shares. Generally, a small advantage can be gained by purchasing rights rather than shares, but this is rarely substantial. Sometimes the market price of the existing shares has been so low that the rights have traded at the purely nominal price of one half of one cent each. Sometimes the price of the shares has fallen to below the take-up price of the rights within a few weeks of the conclusion of the trading in the rights.

Calculating the Price of a Right

In calculating the price of a 'right', two pieces of information are needed: firstly, the number and price of the shares with the rights entitlement and, secondly, the number and price of the shares that one is given the right to purchase. Consider the following information: an investor with ten shares, each with a cum rights price of $2, is given the right to purchase two more shares for $1.50 each. (See Glossary for the meaning of 'cum'.)

Thus for every ten shares bought at $2.00	$20.00
another two can be obtained at $1.50 each	$3.00
Therefore the theoretical price of twelve shares is	$23.00
or approximately $1.92 each.	

The difference between the theoretical 'ex rights' price of the share ($1.92) and the actual price ($1.50) is the price of the right; in this case: 42 cents. Thus 42 cents is the bonus to the investor who holds the shares when the rights issue is announced. This person can either purchase the shares at the discounted price or sell the rights to someone else. Obviously for another investor to buy these rights, the right would have to be priced at something less than 42 cents, otherwise the prospective investor would be indifferent to the choice between purchasing existing shares and 'rights' shares.

Trading in Rights

Should the shareholder want to dispose of his rights, he should, immediately upon receiving his entitlement, put them on the market. There is a tendency for the price of the rights to be highest at the start of trading and to decline towards the end, but again this would depend on the drift of the market.

A few rights issues will be made non-renounceable by the company, which means that there can be no trading in the entitlement. This is at the discretion of the company. As already indicated, some issues of specified preference shares have been made non-renounceable in order to avoid administrative expenses. Rights are not subject to the odd-lot margins, hence a rights issue is a convenient way for a shareholder to complete a parcel of shares that he may hold in the particular company.

Investing in an Initial Flotation

Shares in an initial flotation used to be regarded as a

prize, but these days the premiums demanded have taken the gilt off the gingerbread. It is not normally possible to get shares in an initial flotation unless the investor is an established client of a broker. Even then, not all brokers are given an entitlement to every new flotation on the market. Sometimes the issue has been distributed only to a select few brokers or floated only within a limited geographical area. 'Placements' of shares have also been made. A 'placement' occurs when an entire issue is sold privately to a large investor.

A new flotation is not necessarily to be commended at any price. Sometimes newly issued shares have fallen to a mere fraction of their issue price within a few months of appearing on the market.

One factor is the lack of information about new companies that seek listing and make a flotation. If the company is well established with a secure financial record, then it is to be recommended. But such is not necessarily the case with an unproved new company, which may appear out of the blue.

Despite the soundness of the company, the downward drift of the market may carry the shares down to below their issue price shortly after they begin to trade. The astute investor will know when this is likely to occur, adjusting his buying and selling patterns accordingly. Investors who try to buy shares in a new flotation with the intention of immediately selling them on issue and making a capital gain are known as 'stags'. This sometimes works, but in recent years the capital gains have not been very substantial.

Given that new shares often rise to above their issue price immediately they start to trade, and then, as initial demand falls away, go back to a general market price, it may pay to wait a while before purchasing to see the normal market price of the shares.

Investing in Convertible Notes and Shares

Redeemable notes and shares are now a feature of the Australian sharemarket. These trade in much the same way as the ordinary shares, but have some distinctive features worth noting. Generally, they do not trade as readily as the ordinary shares, and may 'stick' at the optimum time for disposal.

Care is essential before taking up such securities or purchasing them on the market. Note carefully the conditions of issue. Securities of this nature are primarily issued to serve the financial structure of the company and not the interests of the investors. Study especially the conditions under which the shares are redeemed. If they do not convert into other shares, but can be redeemed by the company only in cash, then they are probably little better than fixed-term securities. If there is an option, which is quite frequently the case, to redeem in cash or in other shares, the investor should ensure that he can exercise this option when it falls due.

Note whether or not bonuses accrue to preference shares. It is usual for bonus issues to accrue, but not to be paid out until the shares convert. If there are accrued bonuses then preference shares could sell at a price higher than the ordinary shares.

Quite frequently, notes and preference shares do not convert into ordinary shares on a one-for-one ratio. The conversion rate should be considered before investing in them. Work out a notional conversion prior to taking up these shares in order to compare their price with the current market price of those into which they convert. On the other hand, as these securities frequently sell at a very low price, in some cases below par, they provide a good yield where the investor is sure that he can hold them until they convert. As the conversion date approaches, they will increase to obtain parity with the shares into which they convert.

Chapter Ten
Investment Analysis: 1

So far in this book we have talked generally about the factors which should be considered before a share purchase or sale decision. In this and the next chapter we shall discuss the specific techniques and tools of two particular investment strategies: firstly, the fundamental strategy and, in the next chapter, the technical investment strategy.

Fundamental Analysis

The objective of a fundamental strategy is to ascertain an approximation of a share's intrinsic value. Having done this, the fundamentalist compares this with the market price. If the intrinsic value is sufficiently above the market price, a fundamentalist will buy shares. If the intrinsic value is below the market price he will sell any shares he has.

A fundamentalist arrives at an intrinsic value by use of ratios and percentages calculated from the financial information released by companies (discussed later in this book). Before reviewing the more important of these ratios, it is well to remember that because of time lags between the end of a financial period and the release of information on company performance over that period, all of the calculations are necessarily based on historical data. It is important to remember this, for while history can be a reasonable guide to the future, it cannot be an absolutely reliable barometer.

Bearing this last point in mind, consider the following ratios:

1. *Earnings per share (EPS)*
This is one of three ratios that appear regularly in the 'Stockmarket Statistics' published by the *Australian Stock Exchange Journal*. Its appearance is recognition of its importance both to analysts and investors. The rationale for calculating earnings on a per-share basis follows from stockmarket practice of quoting prices on a per-share basis. The formula for calculating EPS is as follows:

$$\frac{\text{Net Profit Available for Ordinary Shareholders}}{\text{Number of Ordinary Shares Issued}}$$

If the number of ordinary shares issued changes over the space of a year, an average is usually taken.

In an earlier chapter we mentioned the importance of assessing the growth of a firm. Analysing a series of EPS ratios is well suited to this task. It is worth noting, however, that EPS ratios do not permit any meaningful profitability comparison between companies. This is because it is possible for companies with the same dollar amount of share capital to have the make-up of this share capital differ. It is possible, for example, for two companies to have different par values for their shares. Accordingly the denominator in the formula will change, resulting in meaningless information for the purposes of inter-company comparison.

2. *Price/Earnings Ratio (P/E ratio)*
A ratio based on earnings that does permit inter-company and inter-industry comparison is the price/earnings ratio. Along with the dividend yield and dividend coverage ratios (explained later) the price/earnings ratio makes a regular appearance in the sharemarket reports produced by a number of newspapers, including two national dailies, the *Australian* and the *Australian Financial Review*. This pattern is similarly reflected in newspapers in other parts of the world, including the United States of America.

As the name suggests, this ratio is a derivative of the current selling price of a share and the earnings of a share. The calculation is as follows:

$$\frac{\text{Current Selling Price of an Ordinary Share}}{\text{Earnings Per Share for Last Financial Year}}$$

If a share currently sells for $5 and its earnings for the last financial year are 50 cents per share, then its P/E ratio is 10 ($5 ÷ ·50). This means that the ordinary share of this company is selling for ten times its earnings.

The P/E fluctuates with the price of a share, which in turn is influenced by such things as investor confidence, future expectations, the inflation rate, and prevailing interest rates. Generally, investors will pay a high price for shares in companies whose earnings have been growing and are expected to continue in the same way. A comparison of P/E ratios of companies in the same industry will sometimes reveal a share that is underpriced vis-à-vis shares of other companies in the industry.

Alternatively, it could be said that shares with a high P/E are overpriced, and the selling price of those shares could be more prone to fall in the event of a market downturn. The P/E ratio, then, is a useful tool to use in conjunction with other market indicators in making decisions as to whether to buy or to sell shares. Remember, the P/E ratio (sometimes known as the P/E multiple) is usually calculated on historical data (the past financial year) and therefore can only be a guide as to what is a reasonable share price — **NOT** a guarantee.

The P/E ratio frequently appears in another format referred to as an 'Earnings Yield'. In this format it is more often expressed as a percentage. The basic difference in format arises from the inversion of the denominator and numerator of the P/E ratio. The stock exchange publishes a series of such ratios, which are linked to the ASE indices. The series is calculated weekly to two decimal places.

3. *Dividend Per Share (DPS)*

Because dividends represent the portion of earnings made available to the investor, ratios calculated in respect of these amounts become particularly important for those investors primarily interested in short-term income gains. Like the EPS ratio this is calculated on a per-share basis as follows:

$$\frac{\text{Dividends paid to Ordinary Shareholders}}{\text{Number of Issued Ordinary Shares}}$$

Again, for the same reason that the EPS ratio cannot be used to compare companies, namely because of the possibility of different compositions in the share capital, a DPS ratio is similarly affected. In other words, it can be used only to assess the growth of dividends in one company. Despite this drawback the DPS ratio is considered to be of some importance. This importance is borne out by its appearance in the 'Stock Market Statistics' published by the *Australian Stock Exchange Journal*.

4. *Dividend Yield*
The dividend yield, like the earnings yield, is the subject of a stock exchange series, and is linked to the ASE indices. Again, like the earnings yield, it is published weekly to two decimal points, being most commonly expressed as a percentage. The dividend yield is also calculated and reported on a company and industry basis. These figures appear daily in the national newspapers and monthly in the stock exchange publication *Comparative Analysis*.

The dividend yield is calculated as follows:

$$\frac{\text{Dividend Per Share}}{\text{Market Price of Share}} \times \frac{100}{1}$$

Consider the following information:

	(i)	(ii)
Dividend Per Share	10c	30c
Current Share Price	$1.50	$1.50
∴ Dividend Yield	6.7%	20%

Comparison of the two cases above reveals that the

second investment opportunity is by far the better, especially for those investors interested in high yields as opposed to possible capital gains. Among other things, however, this situation may also alert fundamentalists to the possible under-valuation or over-valuation of shares in the market. Depending upon anticipated movements in the market, these calculations may also lead to the buying and selling of shares. For example, if the market appears to be in a downward drift, the 'fundamentalist' will be prone to sell shares with the lowest dividend yields, anticipating a downward movement in the market price to result in a more competitive dividend yield.

5. *Times Dividend Covered*
For those investors interested in the continuity of current income, a times dividend covered ratio is calculated. This ratio features in the statistics published each weekday by the *Australian Financial Review*. It is also easily compiled from the basic company information published in the *Australian Stock Exchange Journal*. The calculation is as follows:

$$\frac{\text{Tax Paid Profits} - \text{Less Preference Dividends}}{\text{Total Amount of Ordinary Dividends Paid}}$$

Consider the following information:

Tax Paid Profits less Preference
　Dividends　　　　　　　　　　　$100,000
Total Amount of Ordinary
　Dividends Paid　　　　　　　　　$20,000
∴ Dividend Cover = 5

This example indicates that dividends are covered five times, which is quite high. Often companies will pay out no more than one-third of profits as dividends. In these situations, dividends will be covered three times. This is not, however, a standard rule. Dividend payout varies according to stability of profits, the need for new capital, and the prospects of future profits. Given that some companies (especially those in their infancy) are likely to have a low dividend payout in order to fund expansion, investors should be careful not to write off such companies too soon. Short-term gains are not always to be preferred to long term.

6. *Net Tangible Asset Backing (NTA)*
This ratio is seldom absent from any stockmarket statistics. It is calculated as follows:

Ordinary Shareholders' Funds Less Intangible Assets[1]
Number of Issued Ordinary Shares

The NTA ratio indicates the financial soundness of a company. Some see it as an indication of the amount of money an ordinary shareholder would receive in the event of liquidation. It is worth noting, however, that as assets are usually stated at their 'historical' cost value, the NTA ratio will usually be fairly conservative. A realistic NTA ratio would necessitate assets being stated at their approximate market value.

Although it is not possible to test whether assets have been valued at market price from the information printed in various newspapers, this is possible from information contained within the *Stock Exchange Journal*. Alongside the column where the NTA ratio is, another column describes shareholders' equity as a percentage of the total equities of the company. Where this figure is accompanied by the letter 'g', this means that investments have been stated at their market value. As a rule, where this occurs the NTA ratio is noticeably higher.

General

Although the ratios and percentages mentioned constitute the major published sharemarket statistics, they are only a few of the possible statistics to which an investor might turn to attempt to estimate the intrinsic value of a company's shares. The statistics described

---
1. e.g. goodwill.

above deal mainly with the profitability of firms. However, other statistics are available to assess the efficiency with which companies use the funds available to them as well as to assess the short-term and long-term survival of companies. Regrettably this book has not the space to deal with any of these. We therefore refer the reader to the literature of accounting, which deals with these issues simply but thoroughly. In doing so, however, we express a note of caution lest the reader cannot see the wood for the trees. A fundamentalist, like any other information-seeker, cannot digest every item of information about a company. Of necessity, some discretion in choosing information must be used. We therefore suggest that the investor concentrate his efforts, at least to begin with, on the ratios and percentages specifically mentioned.

Chapter Eleven
Investment Analysis: 2

Technical Investment Strategy

Perhaps the most conspicuous feature of the technical investment strategy is the almost naïve trust that those who adhere to it place in the capacity of the sharemarket and share prices to reflect the true worth of a share. This trust is reflected in the fact that the technicians maintain that all of the aforementioned fundamental factors are instantly reflected in a share's price on the sharemarket.

Technicians also believe that the past trend of prices falls into an identifiable and recurrent pattern from which predictions about future price movements can be made. The task of the technician therefore is to 'chart' share price movements to identify a pattern of price and/or volume changes. Decisions to buy or sell shares will then be made in light of the economic premise that prices rise when demand exceeds supply (of shares) and vice versa.

Tools of the Technician

The technical analyst makes extensive use of graphs or charts to study the movement of share prices. Charts enable the investor to see readily the way a share price is moving. In addition to charts, the technical analyst also uses mechanical rules in deciding whether to buy or sell shares. More often these mechanical rules will be used after visually identifying a price trend on charts.

Charting

Charting is conducted at two basic levels. At the first level it is carried out for the purpose of trying to gauge the future performance of the general market. At the second level it is conducted to analyse the performance of individual shares.

At the first level the chartist would attempt to graph the movement in stock exchange indices, especially the composite indices. In Australia this would mean graphing an index like the all ordinaries index. Such a graph might look like the one in Figure 1, where time is graphed on the horizontal axis and movement in share prices on the vertical axis.

Notice the identification and matching of events to rises and falls in the graph. The technical analyst believes that a store of such knowledge helps one to predict how the market will move in reaction to certain anticipated events. He further believes that, once in motion, these movements will persist for some period enabling detection and advantageous share trading.

Having predicted the probable future performance of the general market, the technical analyst turns his attention to predicting the movement of individual shares. He does so on the understanding that history repeats itself, and thus historical trends and patterns in share price movements will be repeated.

Although several charting techniques are available to him, the two oldest and most widely used are 'Point-and-figure Charting' and 'Bar Charting'.

1. *Point-and-figure Charting*
The main features of this type of charting are that:
    (i) it is frequently compiled with no time dimension,
    (ii) it disregards small changes in share price, and
    (iii) it requires a share's price to reverse a predetermined number of points before a directional change is recorded.

In Figure 2 we have included a time dimension. The basic unit change in this graph is 2 cents. Unless the price changes by at least 2 cents no movement will be

Figure 1

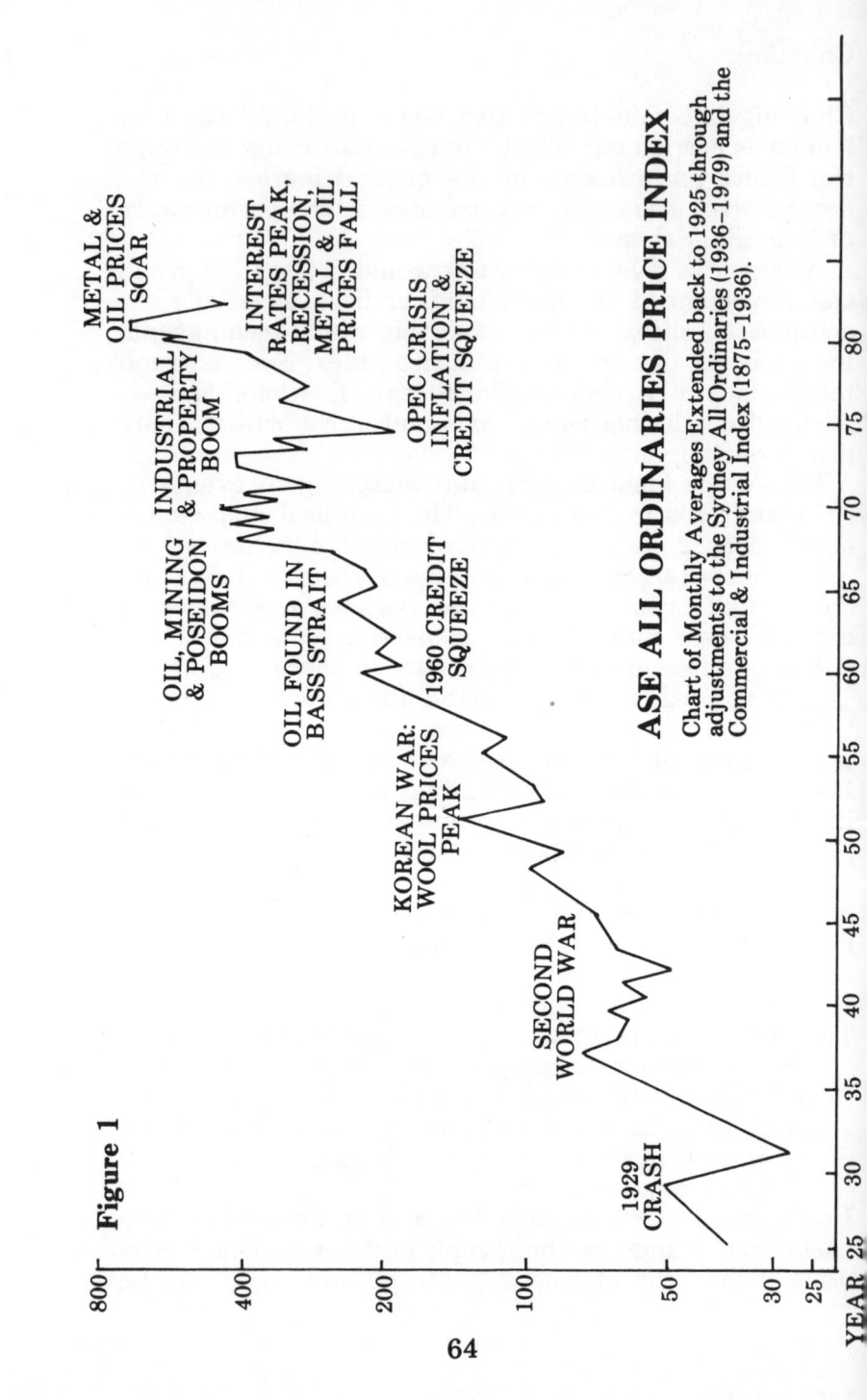

recorded. The crosses indicate upward movements and the small circles downward movements in share price. Given that each one of the points on the horizontal axis represents a period of four days (calculated by dividing a month's trading days (twenty) by the 5 points within a month), it is apparent that at the end of the first four days of trading in September 1981 the share had moved 8 points from 188 to 204. It then fell back to 190 by the end of the last day of trading in September.

A substantial number of patterns and rules have been developed by technicians in respect of point-and-figure charts. For example, references are made to congestion areas, that is, areas in which there are a succession of rallies and reverses precluding any lengthy vertical columns. The width of such an area is said to give the technician some insight into the probable size and direction of a movement by a share to some particular price.

Notwithstanding any argument about the use of such information it seems worth noting that if enough people acted in accordance with point-and-figure information, the prophecies of the charts could well become self-fulfilling.

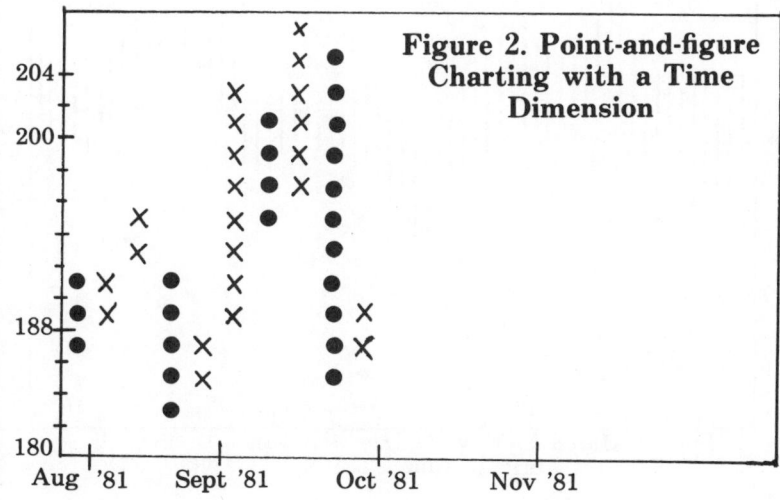

Figure 2. Point-and-figure Charting with a Time Dimension

2. Bar Charting

This type of charting is most prevalent in Australia. A monthly publication, entitled the *Datronics Chart Book*, contains charting information for a number of ASE indices as well as about 400 individual shares. This publication is available at a $40 a month subscription or, alternatively, photocopies of charts of individual companies are available at $2.50 per chart.

The vertical axis of a bar chart usually reflects the share price while the horizontal axis is made up of various time periods. On a bar chart the analyst makes use of a vertical line, the high and low points of which represent the high and low prices of a share over a determined period. In Figure 3 we have portrayed such a chart.

Bar chartists, like point-and-figure chartists, have developed patterns to look for when trying to determine the most probable price action of a stock. Listed below are five patterns that seem to fit most shares despite the kind of market one is in.

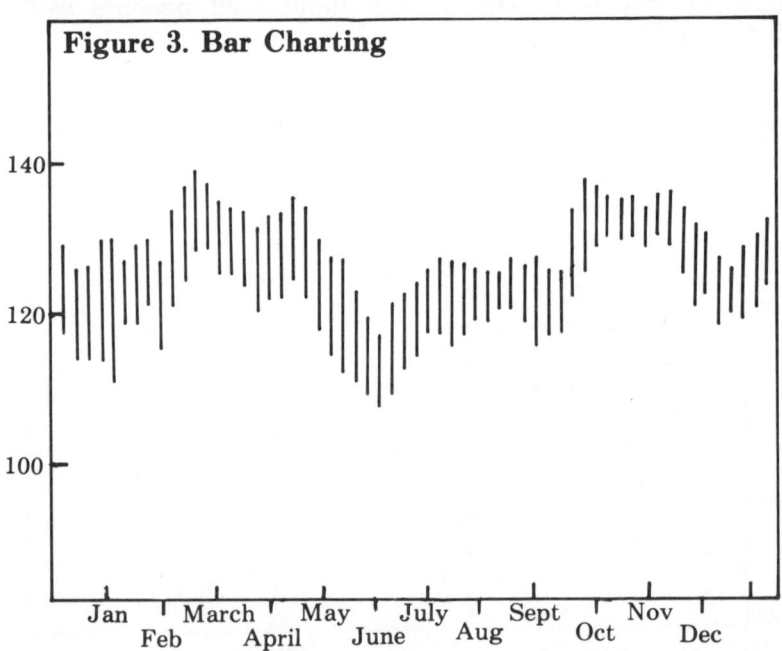

Figure 3. Bar Charting

Figure 4. Five Standard Chart Patterns

	Shares that have performed relatively well in the past, but are currently in a 'stationary' position.
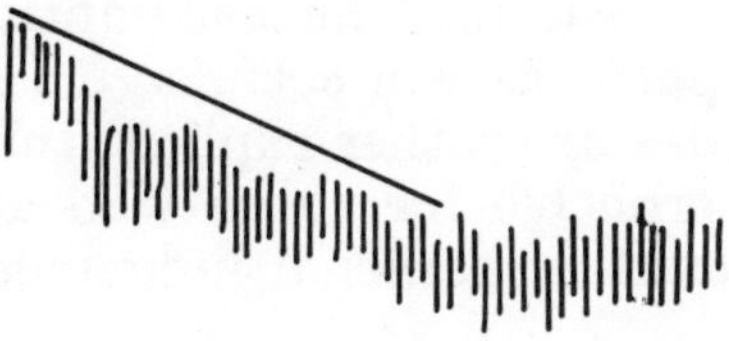	Shares that have declined, but which have subsequently consolidated and offer promise in a favourable market.
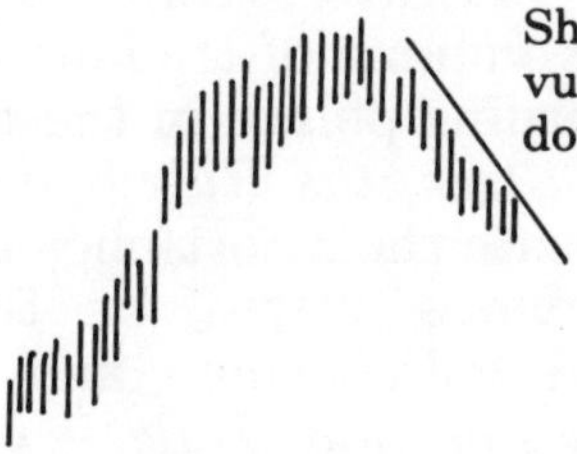	Shares that are in a vulnerable position with downward tendencies.
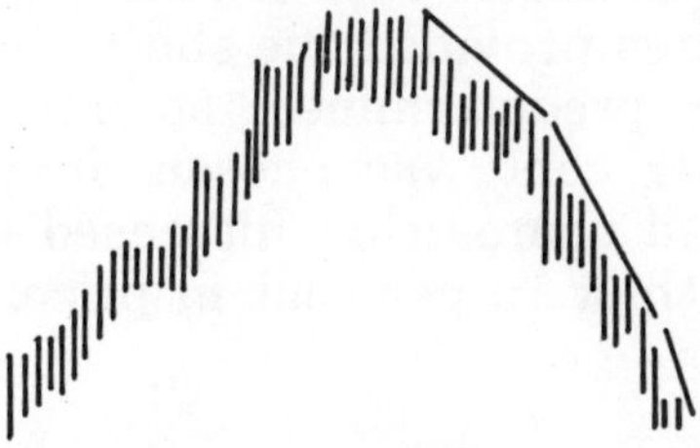	Shares that appear to have reached their lows, but still somewhat vulnerable given the lack of consolidation.
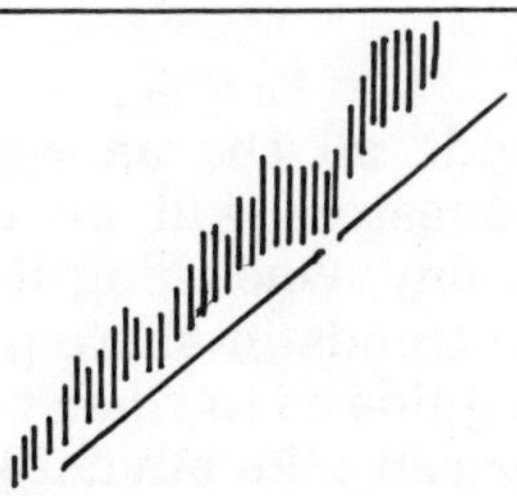	Shares with established upward trends that show few signs of abating.

Mechanical Rules

For those investors unconvinced by the mathematical approach of the fundamentalists and similarly unconvinced by the graphs of the technicians a compromise may be worth considering. In the development of so-called mechanical rules, information that would normally be plotted on graphs is arranged into arithmetical formulas. These formulas are based on patterns of past data that showed profitable results. The assumption with their use is that such patterns will occur again in the future. Because these rules are rather explicit, they tend to offer a suitable alternative for those who are concerned by the large amount of personal judgement involved in chart reading.

Some of the more common rules include:
   (i) *The Leading Indicators Rule* — where various statistics (e.g. volume of trading, money supply) lead major turning-points in the market.
  (ii) *The Relative Strengths Rule* — where investors regularly relocate their portfolios to invest in the better-performance shares, on the assumption that the trend will continue, and
 (iii) *The Arbitrary Formulas Rule* — where investors after choosing a particular rate of change, agree to buy or sell shares provided the share changes in price by the predetermined amount. For example, if 10 per cent was chosen, investors would buy and sell shares that increased or decreased by more than 10 per cent in price.

Summary

Technical analysis cannot provide all the answers in portfolio management. Some investors will no doubt question whether it can provide any. One thing it does do, however, is identify *ex poste* trends in share prices. If in this respect it can provide a guide as to when to buy or sell shares so that an investor can take advantage of clearly discernible trends in a share's price then technical analysis could be a valid investment-decision tool. One last point to be wary of is the extent of support for technical analysis. Irrespective of the deficiencies in technical analysis, the greater the support for it, the more likely the share price is to move in the direction predicted. This, as we suggested earlier, takes on the appearance of a self-fulfilling prophecy.

Chapter Twelve
Sharemarket Indices

Introduction

When investors discuss investments they inevitably talk about movements in the sharemarket. Often these discussions include comments and comparisons of sharemarket movements with the level of liquidity (money supply) in the economy, the trend of public company profits, export receipts for our major export products, and the inflation rate.

Share indices provide a model of sharemarket behaviour. When presented in graph form, share price indices have a special place in the decision framework of regular investors. Indices enable the investor to compare movements in the market with the price movement of individual shares. This latter comparison helps investors decide whether to hold, buy, or sell a shareholding. This comparison of movements in the sharemarket in general with movements in the price of individual shares is an important aspect of modern portfolio management.

The remainder of this chapter describes the major indices compiled in Australia, as well as some in the USA and the United Kingdom.

Objective of Share Price Indices

The aim of a share price index is to summarize the price changes of a range of shares over a specified period of time. In its simplest form such an index represents an historical record of how the market, or sections of it, reacted to past events. Such knowledge is invaluable to those who are predisposed to act on and react to such information. At one end of the spectrum such information can be useful to macro-economic policy makers, such as government, who may use the information as a guide to general business expectations. Such information may also be useful to individuals trying to determine the correct timing of share sales and purchases.

More sophisticated share price indices, which include composite indices (a summary of a number of indices) and accumulation indices, may be used for slightly different purposes. Accumulation indices, for example, reveal the total return on equities over a period of time, thus allowing the investor to measure portfolio performance or the performance of an individual share.

In order to establish the validity of an index for a particular purpose, some knowledge of how the index is calculated and its objective is necessary. While it is not our intention to discuss the technical aspects of index creation in detail, there are three areas that require some explanation. It is in these areas that most of the conflicts between the use and interpretation of different indices arise.

1. *Selection of Companies*
'Selection of companies' encompasses the number and composition of stocks included in an index. Traditionally, computational problems have resulted in the construction of indices based on restricted samples of companies. However, with the development of computers this is now no longer a problem. All eligible companies may now theoretically be included in an index. This in itself presents a problem, however, for an all-company index will include shares that are infrequently traded and therefore incorporate prices that may be unrealistic in the light of changing market conditions.

In the case of a sample-based index, the choice of the sample is very important. The usefulness of a sample is limited to the degree to which movements in the included stocks can be used to infer movements in the excluded stocks. If the sample is of a sufficient size and randomly chosen, there will be a high degree of correspondence, but if the sample reflects a certain category of stocks, say the largest companies, then the relationship is unlikely to be as strong.

2. *Weighting*

This covers the method used to determine the relative importance of each stock included in the index. There are two major methods, the choice of which should be related to the purpose of the index. The first is to weight for market values, i.e. each company is weighted according to the number of shares it has on issue. The second method is that of equal weighting. In this method the assumption is that an equal amount is invested in each stock and thus relative price changes are ranked equally.

In both of the above, adjustments must be made for any capital changes. A bonus issue should have no impact on the relative importance of a particular stock because the increase in the number of shares on issue is, in theory, countered by an off-setting decline in market price. A cash issue, however, does change the overall capitalization of a company, and thus an adjustment needs to be made to accommodate this change.

3. *Method of Averaging*

This is an area of considerable statistical debate. As an index is a means of expressing a group of values as a single descriptive measure, some method of averaging is required. The alternatives are either the geometric or arithmetic mean. The method used will have some impact on the eventual value of the index. Generally, an index based on the geometric mean will increase more slowly and decrease more rapidly than an index based on the arithmetic mean.

As a measure of portfolio performance a share price index using an arithmetic averaging method is regarded as being the more satisfactory measure. All share price indices in Australia are calculated using the arithmetic average.

Australian Share Price Indices

Until January 1980 both the Melbourne and Sydney stock exchanges produced a concurrent set of share price indices. In January 1980, however, these two sets of indices were replaced by a combined set of indices known as the Australian stock exchange (ASE) indices.

Four reasons have been suggested for this change. Firstly, the dramatic change in the composition of the sharemarket. For example, resource-based stocks, which accounted for approximately 10 per cent of the value of shares on the market in the 1950s, increased to 60 per cent by the 1980s. Secondly, the diversification of many leading industrial companies into the resources industry. Thirdly, the introduction of computers, which made possible the timely compilation of indices covering all sectors of the market. And, fourthly, the introduction and adoption in the 1970s of new rules and services for both the Sydney and Melbourne exchanges. Listed on the following page are the indices that are and were covered in the three major groupings. Index numbers 1-24 comprise what are known as the sub-indices, and numbers 27-31 the composite indices.

SHARE PRICE INDICES FOR THE ASE
SYDNEY AND MELBOURNE SERIES

Index Number	Index Name	ASE Indices	Sydney Indices	Melbourne Indices
1	Metals		N	N
2	Solid Fuels		N	N
3	Oil & Gas			
4	Dev & Contractors			
5	Building Materials			
6	Elect. H/hold Durables			
7	Alcohol & Tobacco		N	N
8	Food, H/hold Goods		S	S
9	Textiles, Clothing			
10	Automotive		S	S
11	Chemicals			S
12	Light Engineering		N	N
13	Heavy Engineering		N	N
14	Paper & Packaging			
15	Banks & Finance			
16	Insurance		N	N
17	Retail			
18	Merchants, Agents		N	N
19	Transport		S	S
20	Media			
21	Property Trusts		N	N
22	Other Services		N	N
23	Misc./Diversified Industrial		N	N
24	Diversified Resources		N	N
25	Spare Index Number			
26	Spare Index Number			
27	Metals & Minerals			
28	All Resources		N	N
29	All Industrials			N
30	All Ordinaries			
31	50 Leaders			S

N = No comparable group in Sydney/Melbourne series
S = Major sample differences compared with ASE index

The relationship between the indices is as follows:

Sub-Indices	Composite Indices	
Index Numbers 1 to 3 + 24	= All Resources	
Index Numbers 4 to 23	= All Industrials	} = All Ordinaries

Basically an index is calculated by multiplying a percentage change in the aggregate market value (AMV) of shares at the end of a period of trading by an accepted base figure (usually 500). This percentage change in AMV is calculated by dividing the closing AMV by the opening AMV. For example, if $1000 worth of shares decreases to $900 during a trading session, an index figure of 500 would decrease to 450. This is calculated thus:

Opening Index (×) Change in Aggregate Market Value of Shares Within an Index Group = Closing Index

$$500 \times \frac{900}{1000} = 450$$

Frequency of Calculation
ASE indices are calculated daily in three series. These are:
  (i) The daily price indices (calculated every evening).
  (ii) The daily accumulation indices (calculated every evening).
  (iii) The on-line price indices (calculated throughout the day).

Both the daily price and accumulation indices are available to the public the following morning, while, as one might expect, the on-line index is instantaneously available. Further summary information is available in the *Australian Stock Exchange Journal*, where monthly averages and monthly highs and lows are reported.

A price index is calculated by multiplying the percentage change in aggregate market value of a group of shares with an opening index. An accumulation index is similar except that where dividends are paid, the dividend is added to the closing AMV of shares so as to affect the percentage change in the AMV of shares. The accumulation indices are thus thought to give an indication of total portfolio performance (capital gains plus income) as opposed to share price indices, which only indicate price movements or possible capital gains. On-line indices are constructed only in respect of share price movements, and as suggested earlier are recalculated every time there is a change in the market value of an index stock.

ASE Index Sampling, Weighting, and Averaging

1. *Sample*
The sample upon which ASE indices are based is updated annually on the first day of trading in July. To be eligible for inclusion, a company must have its ordinary shares listed for twelve months preceding the review date. Of these companies 30 per cent will form the sample. This 30 per cent is made up of the top 10 per cent of companies who automatically qualify, and the next 20 per cent who qualify by having had their shares traded in the last ten out of twelve months. A company's ranking is determined on the basis of the amount of issued ordinary capital that a company has at the date of review.

With one exception the bottom 70 per cent of companies together with those from the 20 per cent that do not meet the trading requirements are usually excluded. The exception arises where the sample group (usually between 250 and 280 companies) comprises less than 80 per cent of the AMV of share capital in an index. Companies will be added until this latter requirement is met.

2. *Weighting and Averaging*
The ASE indices were introduced in 1980 on the rec-

ommendation of the Institute of Actuaries of Australia. This body was commissioned by the stock exchange in 1977. Among its recommendations, which were adopted with only minor modifications, it suggested that arithmetic averaging and market value weighting be adopted in preference to the alternatives of geometric averaging and equal weighting. The use of these alternatives is consistent with the construction of major indices in other countries.

Other Stock Exchange Indices

Two other indices have been regularly calculated by the stock exchange since 1972. These are the Statex-Actuaries Indices, developed jointly by the Institute of Actuaries of Australia and the Statex Department of the Sydney Stock Exchange, and the Statex-Actuaries Accumulation index. These indices are based on a common portfolio sample of fifty companies. For more information on the construction of these indices refer to *The Australian Stock Exchange Indices*, a publication of AASE.

Some Selected Overseas Indices

1. The Dow Jones Industrial Average
The Dow Jones is described as an unweighted average of thirty industrial stocks. The term 'unweighted' is something of a misnomer in that the influence of a particular stock is proportional to its price, e.g. a $20 stock is relatively more important than a $10 stock and as a consequence a 10 per cent change in the price of the $20 stock will have twice the impact of a 10 per cent change in the $10 stock *regardless* of the number of shares on issue. The Dow Jones includes stocks that make up approximately 25 per cent of the total market capitalization of stocks listed on the New York Stock Exchange.

A major criticism of the Dow Jones is that the average cannot show relative changes in the way a conventional index does. Also, the thirty companies it includes are all well established and are therefore a rather narrow sample of the overall market.

2. *Standard and Poor's Index*
This is an index comprising 500 stocks listed on the New York Stock Exchange, weighted according to their AMV. Approximately 80 per cent of the market's total capitalization is represented.

The objective of the Standard and Poor's Index is to reflect the change in share prices as a result of market movements and not changes resulting from share issues. Consequently, adjustments for capital movements are made in such a way as to offset the latter.

3. *Financial Times Index*
First calculated in July 1935 at a base index figure of 100, this index comprises thirty equal weighted stocks listed on the London Stock Exchange. These make up approximately 30 per cent of the market's total capitalization.

As with the Standard and Poor's Index, the *Financial Times* Index does not take account of issue related changes in value. It is designed to recognize underlying market movements only.

4. *Financial Times-Actuaries' Index*
This index, comprising 594 weighted stocks listed on the London Stock Exchange, covers approximately 60 per cent of the market's total capitalization. It is designed to take account of all price changes that are issue related and is therefore different to the *Financial Times* Index.

Conclusion

As no single index will ever be ideal for all applications, an understanding of the objectives and method of construction of each will aid in assessing its relevance to a particular situation.

Generally, share price indices have one of two goals.

One is to provide an indication of the movement in share prices resulting solely from market movements. The aim here is to isolate changes that can be related to economic or anticipated economic events. Price movements arising from capital adjustments are ignored. The second approach is to provide a bench-mark for measuring or assessing portfolio performance. In this case the aim is to show how investor wealth has changed over time. Therefore, market induced movements as well as price movements associated with capital changes are recognized.

Unlike many overseas countries, where several groups produce comparable sets of indices, in Australia, with the exception of the fixed-interest securities index produced by the Commonwealth Bank, all indices are produced by the stock exchange. The indices are published in daily, weekly, or monthly stock exchange bulletins and in national daily newspapers, such as the *Australian Financial Review* or the *Australian*.

Chapter Thirteen
Understanding Annual Accounts

In order to make investment decisions, investors require information. One of the ways an investor can acquire information about a firm is by reference to a company's annual accounts. The contents of these accounts are prescribed jointly by law and by other interested bodies, including the stock exchange and the various professional accounting bodies. Fundamental analysis as described in chapter ten is based on the information contained in annual accounts. For this reason some understanding of annual accounts is desirable.

The Companies Act 1981 requires that all public companies present annual financial statements that reflect a 'true and fair' view of the operations and financial position of a company. These statements comprise a balance sheet, a profit-and-loss account, a directors' report, an auditors' report and, if the company is the head of a group of companies, a set of group accounts. Group accounts comprise the combined balance sheet and profit-and-loss accounts of all companies in a group. All people with a financial interest in a company (including shareholders and debenture-holders) are entitled to a free copy of the annual accounts.

The 'listing requirements' of the stock exchange, although not law, have the effect of law as far as listed public companies are concerned. Besides the statements mentioned above and other specific information, public companies that wish to be listed must prepare a statement of source and application of funds as well as half-yearly statements of income and financial position, referred to as 'interim accounts'.

Although in effect companies that are not listed on the exchange are not legally obliged to present a statement of source and application of funds, the practice of so doing is becoming increasingly more common as a result of the regulations of professional accounting bodies in Australia, which requires that all its members comply or face expulsion. Effectively, then, there is a need to explain the workings of at least five statements. First up is the balance sheet.

Balance Sheet

A balance sheet constitutes a two-sided statement showing two basic things. On one side it shows all the goods or property a business owns (assets). On the other side it displays the ownership interests in those assets or all the debts of a business. Basically there are two ownership interests. One is represented by those who actually own shares in the business and the other by those who have lent the company money. Although some dispute surrounds the objective of a balance sheet, basically it is meant to give a snapshot of the financial condition of the business at the end of the financial year, commonly 30 June.

Balance Sheet Preparation

Balance sheets are traditionally prepared from accounting information collected and recorded at historical transaction costs, i.e. purchase price. As such they are not necessarily indicative of the firm's true worth. Accordingly, unless the company has made some effort to revalue its assets (especially its fixed assets) at something approximating current values, care should be exercised when attempting to assess the current worth of a business. If you are in any doubt about whether assets are shown at their realistic current values, look for a date alongside the asset amount. The Companies Act

1981 requires that all fixed assets that have been revalued have the date of their revaluation alongside them. Where no date appears, one may reasonably assume that the asset is stated at its original cost.

The Tie Between the Balance Sheet and the Profit-and-loss Statement

A balance sheet purports to show the financial position or condition of a business on a particular day. Given that a firm's assets help to produce income it is not unreasonable to expect that this position will change from time to time. Assets, for example, will be used up in the production of income. The difference between two balance sheets is the profit or loss for a period. This difference appears as a single figure in the second of two balance sheets. It appears as part of the interests of shareholders. This figure is the subject of considerable explanation in the profit-and-loss statement.

Profit-and-loss Statement

The profit-and-loss statement, like the balance sheet, comprises two items. In this case, however, the items are not assets and liabilities, but revenues and expenses. Revenues denote the inflow of resources into the firm. These resources flow in primarily, but not exclusively, as the result of sales. Expenses denote the outflow of resources.

In order to make sales, businesses have to use up assets (e.g. machinery used to produce goods) and incur costs such as electricity and rent. These latter items constitute expenses. All the revenues and expenses are offset in the profit-and-loss statement to determine a single profit or loss for a period. Once tax has been paid on this profit, it can then be distributed as dividends to shareholders. Any amount not used up is placed into the general funds of the shareholders. As indicated above, this appears as a single figure in the balance sheet.

The Directors' Report

Although the Companies Act once again specifies the need for certain information, traditionally this report (usually devoid of figures) gives a review of the trading results of the year just past. Contained within the report is frequently a statement previewing the ensuing year's trading prospects. A careful reading of the prose in the directors' annual reports can provide useful non-financial data for investment decisions.

The Auditors' Report

An auditor is a person knowledgeable in financial affairs, independent of the company whose financial statements he is reviewing, and who is appointed on behalf of shareholders to attest to the validity of the financial statements. His report attests that the accounts have been compiled on the basis of sound accounting practices. The implication of an unqualified audit report is that information contained in the financial statements is useful for decision-making purposes. Because this report is the only real protection for those not able to assemble or fully understand all the information contained in financial statements, this is an important report.

Funds Statements

Sometimes referred to as a statement of changes in financial position, the funds statement shows where the company acquired its funds during the year, e.g. from operations (net profit) or from selling assets. The statement also shows how the funds that were acquired were used, e.g. for paying dividends or buying other assets. The reason this statement is presented to shareholders is that often the traditional profit-and-loss account and balance sheet do not prove to be meaningful to novice investors, because they do not give clear answers to questions such as: 'Why are we getting such a low dividend when the company has made such large profits?' and 'Why, when the company has made such big profits, has the bank balance gone from a positive amount to an amount in overdraft?'

Although this statement is not required for all companies, its usefulness in terms of answering the above questions has made it a common feature of annual accounts.

Trend Statements

The Companies Act 1981 requires companies to provide comparative figures for the last financial year alongside those of the current year. However, many Australian companies, appreciating the need for a greater amount of investor information, are now presenting five and sometimes ten years' worth of comparative figures. Typically, these statements will contain dollar figures for sales, net profit, dividends, shareholders' funds, income tax, current assets, current liabilities, and many others.

In addition, some firms cater for the need of the fundamentalists by preparing statistics based on these five/ten-year trends. These statistics include 'return on average shareholders' funds', 'current ratio', 'net tangible asset backing per ordinary share', 'dividend yield', and 'earnings per share'.

Trend statements will often prove very helpful to the novice investor, who may find it difficult trying to discern growth patterns of companies from traditional financial statements.

Accounting Jargon

Accountants, like other professionals, have developed an array of technical terms, some of which it may be important for the novice investor to know. The more important of these are included in the glossary at the back of this book. (See Appendix B.)

Chapter Fourteen
Investing in Fixed-Term Securities

Fixed-term Investing

Playing the sharemarket is not a form of investing suited to everybody. An alternative to investing in shares is to invest in fixed-term securities. Fixed-term investing has an advantage over share investing in that it does not require constant attention to share price movements in order to decide whether to buy or sell. Nor does it require anywhere near the same amount of administrative work. Once in his possession the investor can forget about the securities until their maturity date and can lodge them with a solicitor or place them in bank safe custody and arrange for interest and principal, as it falls due, to be paid into a bank account. This obviates much administrative work.

Besides being suitable for those who do not want to be actively concerned on a day-to-day basis with the progress of their investments, certain types of fixed-term investments can also be useful to the active share investor who wants to keep his funds close at hand while awaiting further opportunity to purchase more shares.

With the very high share prices prevailing in recent years, yields on shares have not been substantial, and some investors have been attracted to the interest rates of up to 15 per cent that some fixed-term securities offer.

Authorities Issuing Fixed-term Securities

1. *Commonwealth Government*

If this sort of investment interests you, there are a

number of alternatives open. One alternative is to invest in federal government securities. Two options are available: Commonwealth Bonds and Australian Savings Bonds.

Until recently both options provided attractive investment options for the small investor. However, in July 1982 the system by which Commonwealth Bonds were made available to the public was changed. Previously bonds were more or less continually available, but they are now available for only one-week subscription periods. There were seven such issues in 1982. The method by which the yield is calculated was also changed. It is this latter change that makes the purchase of Commonwealth Bonds unattractive to the small investor.

Under the new system a distinction is made between the small and the large investors. A small investor is one who invests in $1000 units, and a large investor is one who invests in $100,000 units. The new system, referred to as the 'tender' system, permits the large investors effectively to determine the yield of the small investor. When the large investors apply for the bonds, they are permitted (unlike the small investor) to identify the yield they want. They place what is known as a 'competitive bid'. The Commonwealth government, depending upon the amount of money it needs, accepts those tenders who give it the money it needs at the lowest possible interest rates. The various interest rate tenders are then averaged out and that becomes the yield. By this time the small investor (who makes a non-competitive bid) has invested his money and must accept the average yield. In the series 3 of 1982 this actually worked against the small investor. The announced yield by the government on the initial offering of the bonds was 13 per cent. However, because interest rates were falling at the time, a number of competitive bids below the officially announced yield permitted the final yield to be drawn at 12.8%. Small investors had no choice but to accept this yield or sell their bonds, almost certainly at a loss, on the stock exchange. For this reason Commonwealth Bonds no longer appear an attractive investment proposition for the small investor.

By contrast, however, Australian Savings Bonds are attractive. One of the most important considerations when purchasing fixed-term securities is the likely movement of interest rates over the time of the maturity. In this respect a great deal of care should be taken when purchasing fixed-term securities in periods when interest rates are rising. Otherwise investors may find, to their disadvantage, that some time during the maturity period, current interest rates will exceed those of fixed-term securities. The purchase of Australian Savings Bonds provides a hedge against this occurring. Compared to Commonwealth Bonds, which have a minimum maturity of two years, Australian Savings Bonds have a maturity period of thirty days, at the discretion of the investor. With interest rates that are not at the discretion of large investors, and a minimum investment amount of $20 instead of $1000, Australian Savings Bonds are an attractive investment alternative, especially for the small investor.

Two further points about Australian Savings Bonds should be noted. Firstly, they are available in two forms. In one form, known as 'Inscribed Bonds', the purchaser's name is placed on the bond and in order to sell it must be taken into the Reserve Bank so the name on the certificate can be changed. In a second form, described as 'Bearer Bonds', no name is placed on the bonds, in which case they are the equivalent of cash. For obvious reasons, however, a great deal of care should be taken in respect of security for the Bearer Bonds.

Another point about Australian Savings Bonds is that, unlike Commonwealth Bonds, there is no official market for them. There is, however, an unofficial market. This market is conducted by stockbrokers, post offices, and banks.

2. *Semi-government Authorities*
A second form of fixed-term investing is semi-government loans. Semi-government loans include those floated by various state electricity bodies, water boards, gas boards, etc.

3. *Business Organizations*
Finance companies and other general forms of business organizations offer a third form of fixed-term security. Two types of these securities exist: debentures and unsecured notes. Information about these and any new issues of fixed-term securities, together with their individual maturity dates and interest rates, is available every Wednesday in *Fixed Interest Offerings*, a publication of the AASE.

The Term and The Rate of Interest

Fixed-term securities do not carry a dividend, but pay interest over the term of the security. Information in this regard will be noted in the prospectus and on the certificate issued in respect of the security. A summary of all listed securities and their interest rates can be found monthly in the *Australian Stock Exchange Journal* and periodically in some national newspapers. Unlike a dividend, this rate of interest will not generally be raised to accord with company profitability. It is the subject of a contract and will remain the same during the term of the security unless, for some reason, the contract is renegotiated. This is unusual, but it has happened. At least one company has very recently issued debenture securities with a reviewable interest rate.

The rate of interest is the price paid for money lent and, unlike the sharemarket, this is subject to some considerable control. Generally, governments like to keep interest rates at a low level in the belief that high interest rates may stifle growth and be inflationary at the same time. Government has been especially concerned to keep housing finance rates at a low level for social and political reasons.

Even so, interest rates over the past twenty years have steadily increased and now rates of up to 15 per cent on company debenture securities are not uncommon. These long-term trends in interest rates should concern the investor in fixed-term securities, especially when trying to determine how long he will contract to hold such securities. If interest rates are increasing, it is inadvisable to invest in fixed-term securities that have a long period to run, since interest rates could rise during the term and the security will thus yield less than the current rate of interest.

An added problem could arise if the investor dies or for some reason has to sell the security. Should this happen, the sale price of the debenture or government security will be discounted to equate the yield with the current rate of interest. This means in effect that rising interest rates will cause the capital price of the security to diminish. So where interest rates are rising, short-term investing is preferred. On the other hand, if the investor can accurately predict that interest rates will decline during the currency of the security, it would pay to invest long term.

When offering fixed-term security, the borrower will usually offer a variety of maturity dates to select from. Generally, the longer the term the greater will be the rate of interest, but sometimes borrowers have offered higher rates for lesser terms. This could be because for their own financial reasons they need more finance in one particular short-term maturity, or because they feel that, over the long term, interest rates will fall. A borrower will normally offer only an interest rate sufficient to get finance for his needs.

There will be slight differences in rates of interest offered by different borrowers to accord with the differences in the degree of security that they can afford. Thus interest rates on government loans will be lowest because these are the more secure form of fixed-term investment. There is nothing that excels government stock as a gilt-edged security. Semi-government securities will issue at rates slightly above those of federal governments because of the slightly greater risk involved. Note that semi-government includes organizations such as the Department of Main Roads, and the respective state electricity bodies, whose loans are state government guaranteed, and are therefore attractive because they are to all intents and purposes government securities with a slightly higher rate of return. All semi-government securities are relatively risk-free. Except for a few isolated instances, no semi-government body has become bankrupt in Australia.

Limited liability companies listed on the stock exchange offer rates above those of government and local bodies because of the greater risk involved. Unlike government and semi-government authorities, whose rates are set by the Loan Council, a body made up of Commonwealth and state representatives, there is no uniformity in rates offered by companies.

Various other institutions approach the public for finance. These will frequently offer rates above those offered by listed companies in order to attract funds. However, although these rates may appear attractive, a high interest rate usually means a high risk. A number of these fringe borrowers have collapsed in recent years. An investor should always seek financial or legal advice before investing in an unlisted company or any other institution. Remember that no borrower will offer an interest rate above that which is absolutely necessary to enable him to attract the funds he needs.

Some companies, because of their financial position in being able to turn their funds over more rapidly than others, can offer higher interest rates than other companies, with security.

The Sale of Fixed-term Securities

Fixed-term securities can be bought and sold on the sharemarket in much the same way as shares. Prices paid for them will generally equate with the current rates of interest. But the price will also take into account any accrued interest on the security. It is therefore difficult to calculate accurately the current value of any fixed-term security without professional assistance.

To avoid capital loss, a small investor should not as a rule sell fixed-term securities. Accordingly great care should be exercised in their purchase. The investor's financial commitments should ensure that it will not be necessary to liquidate the security during its term. If some doubt exists about this, the company share is a preferable investment. On the other hand, the possibility of a capital gain should prompt the investor to purchase security that has been issued, rather than to invest in an initial flotation. This type of security is not all that readily available, and it may prove difficult for the investor to get a maturity date that suits his needs.

Very-short-term Investing

Sometimes the investor needs accommodation for his funds for a short period, say up to a few months. There is an established short-term money market in Australia in treasury notes and other paper, but this is not designed to suit the small, private investor as much as the commercial community. This is because treasury notes and bank bills are available only in very large denominations, e.g. $50,000 and $100,000. However, there is a way small investors can take advantage of the short-term money market. This financial mechanism is the cash management trust.

Cash Management Trusts

Cash management trusts are a fairly recent addition to the financial scene in Australia. There are approximately fifteen of these financial institutions, and their names — along with their current interest rates — are listed in the national daily newspapers and the *Australian Stock Exchange Journal* under the heading 'Current Interest Rates Table'. These trusts represent a sort of collective of investors who individually do not have sufficient funds to enter the short-term money market. They allow small investors for as little as $1000 to share in the benefits of this type of investment.

The cash management trust also offers a wider range of investment terms than if investors invested in treasury bonds, and whereas treasury bonds normally mature in between 90 and 180 days, investments in cash management trusts can be made on call. In other words, one's investment is returnable, with interest, within twenty-four hours. Some trusts permit monies to be withdrawn at two hours' notice.

For more information about how these institutions operate, and the various investment alternatives they offer, potential investors should make direct contact with the various trusts. Their brochures also list the guarantors of the trusts.

Mortgage Investing

Investing in first mortgages is probably the safest and least arduous form of investment, though less remunerative than other forms of investment. It must be done through a solicitor. The investor merely hands a cheque to a solicitor with the request that it be invested on first mortgage. All documentation will be done by the solicitor, and the client will be charged a collection fee for the interest received from the mortgagee. Income from the mortgages will either be paid to the client or retained and reinvested in further mortgages by the solicitor. Thus the investor has no paper work at all. This form of investing suits elderly people who want to be free of any trouble associated with investing.

Many firms of solicitors now have nominee companies that they use as a vehicle for this form of finance. The nominee company will hold the security as the formal mortgagee.

The rate of interest paid on mortgage finance tends to be somewhat lower than that for other fixed-term security. There is usually a penalty for late payment or, to be more correct, a discount in interest payable if paid before a certain date. When the solicitor's collection fee is taken into account, the return on mortgage investing does not compare well with other forms of investing.

Chapter Fifteen
The Australian Options Market

Up until this point an 'option' has been described simply as a right attached to a share issue that permits the purchaser to take up further shares at some future date at a specified price. In view of developments in the last eight years, in particular the setting up of The Australian Options Market, options can no longer be described so simply.

Prior to the setting up of The Australian Options Market, trading in options was conducted through options brokers and necessitated a contractual tie between the buyer and the seller. With the introduction of The Australian Options Market and the idea of exchange traded (or listed) options, the job of the options broker and the contractual tie between the buyer and seller were eliminated.

Exchange traded options first appeared on the floor of the Sydney Stock Exchange in February 1976. At that time only 'call' options were available. It was not until September 1982 that exchange traded 'put' options were introduced. A 'call' is an options contract giving the purchaser the right to buy shares at a predetermined price before a specified date, whereas a 'put' is an options contract giving the purchaser the right to sell shares at a predetermined price before a specified date. Put and call options are highly versatile instruments, which can be used in many ways to achieve various investment objectives. Trading techniques can range from simply purchasing either a put or call option to engaging in highly sophisticated and complex 'spreading' and 'hedging' strategies.

This new investment medium has many advantages and improvements compared with old style options:

(i) Standardization of expiry dates, exercise prices (otherwise known as the strike price), and the number of shares in a contract (usually 1000).

(ii) Continuous public reporting of option transactions via the stock exchange reporting mechanism.

(iii) The use of a clearing house, Options Clearing House Pty Ltd (OCH), a fully owned subsidiary of The Sydney Stock Exchange Limited, to streamline the processing of options trades and eliminate the requirement of a contractual tie between the buyer and seller of the option.

(iv) Appointment of registered traders who are market professionals required by the exchange to provide a continuous and orderly secondary market in options trading.

Put and Call Options Trading on the Australian Options Market

Put and call options are traded on The Australian Options Market in much the same manner as ordinary securities. Both market and limit orders are permitted. An order arriving at the trading floor is directed to the appropriate post for execution. The price paid for the option is determined by several factors, including supply and demand for the option, the price and volatility of the underlying security, and the period of time remaining before the expiry date of the option. Put and Call options can be both bought and sold, though it is to be noted from the outset that a Call and a Put are not the opposite sides of the same transaction. This is evidenced by the fact that both financial instruments are traded independently of each other.

Reasons for Purchasing Call Options

(a) *In anticipation of an increase in the price of the underlying security.* The ability to profit from the buying of a call option lies in the belief that the price of the underlying stock will increase, resulting in an increase in the call price, so that at some time prior to the expiration the option can be either exercised or sold at a profit. The majority of options buyers elect to sell their options in the market. By purchasing the call, the buyer may be able to participate in an increase in the price of the underlying security by investing a fraction of the total cost of the share, thus obtaining greater returns on his investment than if it was only possible to trade in the underlying security. An example will illustrate this.

On 15 October the ordinary shares of Digby International Ltd (DIL) are selling at $4.00. A DIL March $4.50 call can be purchased for $400 (contract covering 1000 shares at 40 cents premium per share exercisable at $4.50 per share). Two months later, on 15 December, DIL is selling at $4.50 a share and the call with three months to run is trading at 73 cents ($730). If the call is sold and the profit is compared with the profit had the shares (rather than the option) been purchased in October, the following figures would result:

	Call	Share
Bought 15 October	$400	$4000
Sold 15 December	730	4500
Profit	330	500
% Return on Investment	82.5%	12.5%

(b) *As a means of securing a future share price.* Often an investor who is temporarily unable to purchase shares because of a lack of ready cash will seek to secure the shares at a favourable price in anticipation of future cash flows, from the sale of property, for example. To establish the maximum price he will have to pay for the shares, he can purchase call options covering the number of shares that he will be able to purchase in the future. When his cash flow occurs, and if the shares have risen since the purchase of the options, he will exercise his calls and purchase the shares. If the shares have declined in the interim, it will of course make little sense to exercise his option, because he can buy the shares on the ordinary market for less. In respect of the option held, the investor should seek to recover a portion of his outlay costs by selling the call on the secondary market. The amount of the loss to be sustained will depend upon the time remaining and the degree of decline in the price of the underlying security.

Reasons for Purchasing Put Options

(a) *In anticipation of a decrease in the price of the underlying security.* The ability to profit from the buying of a put option lies in the belief that the underlying stock will decrease, resulting in an increase in Put premium so that at some time prior to expiration the option can be either exercised or sold at a profit. Should the underlying security continue to rise instead of decline, the put option buyer must be aware that a total loss of his entire cash outlay may result, but this would normally occur only if he continued to hold the option and it expired worthless. If the option is sold prior to its expiration, part of the premium should be recovered because of the remaining time value.

(b) *As protection against a share price fall.* Another important advantage that the purchase of put options can provide is protection against a possible decline in price of a stock held. This strategy can be particularly useful if the investor anticipates such a decline, but does not wish to sell the stock, believing in the company's long-term potential. Perhaps the investor wishes to preserve a previous share price gain. The purchase of a put option in such circumstances provides the investor with insurance against a fall in the price of the stock.

Selling Both Call and Put Options

Options sellers also have a variety of strategies at their disposal. At any time during the life of the option the seller of a call option is obliged to deliver 1000 shares of the underlying security to the buyer of the option upon receipt of an exercise notice from OCH, in consideration for payment of the exercise (strike) price, while the seller of a put option is obliged to receive 1000 shares of the underlying security upon receipt of an exercise notice from OCH, in consideration of payment of the exercise (strike) price. For assuming this obligation, he is paid a premium at the time he sells (writes) either a put or call option.

A call option buyer would normally be expected to exercise the option only if the market price is above the exercise price of the shares, and in the case of a put option below the exercise price of the shares, and there is little or no time premium left in the option. The seller of a call option, or buyer of a put option, may deliver the securities he is holding, buy the securities in the market, or exercise another call option of the same class to satisfy the delivery.

Although the seller of a call option is obligated to deliver shares, and the seller of a put option is obliged to receive shares against his option during the life of the option, he may at any time prior to being allocated an exercise notice cancel his obligation by buying an option, identical to the one he has sold in a closing purchase transaction. He will incur a loss if he buys at a higher premium than he had sold, or realize a profit if he buys for a premium lower than he had sold. A seller should always be aware of this alternative for liquidating an open option position.

Reasons for Selling Call Options

(a) *In anticipation of a decline in the price of the underlying security* (scrip covered selling). This is the most common and perhaps easiest to understand reason for selling call options. By receiving a premium (the price of the option), the seller intends to realize additional return on the underlying security in his portfolio, or gain some element of protection, limited to the amount of premium less transaction costs, from a decline in the value of the underlying security. In other words, he is willing to forsake possible appreciation in his underlying security in return for payment of the premium. The seller is required to maintain the scrip cover with OCH for the duration of the option.

(b) *In anticipation of making a cash profit without the capital costs of having to buy the underlying securities (cash covered selling)*. The cash covered call option seller hopes to realize income from the selling transaction. Like the scrip covered writer, his maximum profit is the premium received less transaction costs. There is, however, a greater risk involved, which stems from the possibility of a sudden increase in the price of the underlying shares above the exercise price, leading to the possible exercise of the option, which would necessitate the purchase of shares at the higher market price to satisfy delivery. Consider the following example. Shares in ABC Ltd are selling at 80 cents on 3 February, and the call options in September are valued at 40 cents. That is, the shares can be bought in September by the holder of the option at $1. The seller of the option is assuming that at the conclusion of the option's life (in 8 months) that the market price of the underlying shares will be no more than $1.40. If the shares go above $1.40, however, and remain thus until the expiration of the contract, he will lose money, unless of course he can execute a closing purchase transaction in the same series, in which case his loss will depend upon the difference between the cost of the closing transaction and the net proceeds from the original written transaction.

A further point to note in respect of cash covered call selling is that the seller is required to maintain margins and a fixed deposit with the OCH, and in a rising market he will receive daily calls for additional margins, which is another potential cost to take into account.

Only those individuals who fully understand the risks and are prepared to assume the financial obligations attached should invest in this type of contract.

Reasons for Selling Put Options

(a) *In anticipation of acquiring shares at a lower price.* The seller of a put option becomes obligated to purchase the underlying security at any time up to the expiration date, at a predetermined price. An investor who is unwilling to purchase shares in a particular company at the current market price may elect to write put options in the hope of acquiring the stock at a lower price. Should the put be exercised, the cost of the stock will be the exercise price less the premium.

While a similar result may have been achieved by placing a limit order for the particular stock, writing a put option has the advantage that in the event the option is not exercised and the stock is not acquired, at least the premium has been received. Should the investor have chosen to place a limit order and not acquire the stock, he would have received nothing.

Writers of put options *must* appreciate the possibility that they may be required to pay far more than the current market value of the stock that they are acquiring. This would normally happen only if the stock price fell below the exercise price prior to expiration. As previously mentioned, such an obligation to acquire stock may be terminated at any time by purchasing an offsetting put option.

(b) *As a means of generating cash flow.* The investor intending to write put options as a means of generating income by receipt of the option premium must exercise care in selecting the underlying security. Remembering that the possibility always exists that the option may be exercised, an investor should not write a put option against a share that he is not willing to own.

Once the investor has chosen the specific share, he must then decide whether to write a put in which the exercise price is above, below, or equal to the current market value of a share. This decision will depend largely upon his view of the future market prospects of the company's shares. By way of example, let us assume that an investor who is anticipating a near term increase in the price of the underlying share decides to write a put option in which the exercise price is above the current market price of the share, in order to earn a larger premium. If as anticipated, the share price rises above the exercise price, it is most unlikely the option would be exercised and the premium received for the option would be retained.

It should be remembered, however, that while a put option with a higher exercise price results in a greater premium, it also increases the possibility of exercise.

Additional Strategies

The number and variation of strategies that can be accomplished by using a combination of both put and call options is virtually limitless. There is, however, one such strategy that bears mentioning. It is known as a 'straddle' and can be defined as the simultaneous buying (or writing) of an equivalent number of put and call options in the same underlying security with the same exercise price and expiration date.

1. *Buying a Straddle.*
An investor who believes there is likely to be a substantial price movement in a particular stock, but is unsure of the direction, may seek to profit regardless of the direction of the price change by buying a straddle. A profit will be realized provided that at any time during the life of the option the share price either rises or falls sufficiently to result in the total premiums at that time exceeding the total premiums originally paid. Should the share price fail to move sufficiently in either direction the most the investor can lose is the cost of the options.

2. *Writing a Straddle.*
Whereas a straddle is usually bought by an investor who expects a significant movement in the price of the under-

lying share, a straddle is written by the investor who does not anticipate such a significant price movement. Provided the price of the share remains within a range of the exercise price plus or minus the total premium, the writer of a straddle will realize a profit.

Summary
The example of option strategies presented here are intended to acquaint readers with the most common uses and applications of listed options. They are not meant to exhaust all possibilities, for there are many variations of option strategies and spreading combinations. The following booklets published by Options Clearing House will provide further information of exchange traded options and are available from your broker or the Stock Exchange bookshop:

> *Understanding Options*
> *Dealing in Options*
> *Options: The Versatile Investment*
> *An Introduction to Put Options*

Chapter Sixteen
Taxation

All companies in Australia pay tax on their net profits at the rate of 46 cents in the dollar. However, realized capital profits, such as the increase in value of assets held, are not subject to taxation.

Dividends paid to shareholders from company net profits are aggregated with other sources of personal income — such as salary and interest — and personal income tax is levied at the appropriate rate. Rates of personal income tax are as follows:

$1 — $ 4595	NIL
$ 4596 — $19,500	30 cents/dollar
$19,501 — $35,788	46 cents/dollar
$35,789 and over	60 cents/dollar

Given that companies pay a tax on their net profits and that shareholders are taxed on the dividends they receive from companies, it is apparent that company profits attract a double tax. Consider the following example. Assuming a company has $1 in profits and distributes it all after paying taxes the after tax return to individuals facing different marginal tax brackets is as follows:

Profit	$1.00
Tax	0.46
Dividend	0.54

MARGINAL TAX RATE	DIVIDEND	AFTER TAX RETURN
NIL	54c	54c
30c	54c	38c approx.
46c	54c	29c "
60c	54c	22c "

From the above it is apparent that the higher the marginal tax rate an investor must endure, the smaller is his overall return from company profits.

Profits realized on the sale of shares are usually not subject to income tax in the hands of the investor. However, if an investor regularly buys and sells shares, section 26(a) and in particular 26AAA may be invoked.

Briefly, section 26(a) requires the inclusion in a taxpayer's assessable income of any profit arising from a sale transaction involving any property acquired for the purpose of sale. Section 26AAA brings in as assessable income any income arising from the sale of property within twelve months of its purchase. Exceptions to section 26AAA are granted at the commissioner's discretion, where it can be shown that any income earned was not the primary purpose of the sale transaction.

In terms of the above subsection it is currently the department's policy to treat as assessable income profits that arise from transactions where there is *habitual dealing*, that is, when the taxpayer habitually deals in shares with a view of making a profit on their resale; or *intention*, that is, where there is an obvious intention at the time of purchase of the shares to resell at a profit.

Chapter Seventeen
Sources of Information

The information contained in this book is of a broad nature, designed to provide a background to investment. It does not, nor did it seek to, provide information about any one company. Accordingly, more company and market-specific information will be required to enable investment decisions to be made.

The following is a selection of some of the sources of information available to the investor. For convenience, we have separated these sources according to how regularly the information is provided — instantaneously, daily, weekly, monthly, annually, and periodically.

Instantaneous Information

1. *On-line Share Price Indices*
Instantaneous information is available from two sources — the stock exchange and one's broker. The information from the stock exchange is made available through three mediums: the public address system, the stock exchange Translux screens, and a telephone service. The public address system advises on general developments in the market such as large sales of a particular stock, while the Translux screens detail information in respect of the on-line share price indices. These indices are recalculated and available minute by minute as bids change and shares are bought and sold. The telephone service, which is maintained in each state and updated throughout the day, acquaints any caller with the most recent stocks traded, as well as a summary of the number of share

prices that have risen and fallen. A list of each state's phone numbers for this service is given in Appendix C.

2. *Stockbrokers (Sharebroker)*
The second source of instantaneous information is via one's broker. The professional reputation of a broker is built in part on his fingertip knowledge both of the market in general and particular shares within the market. Information from such a broker is instantaneous in the sense that it is little more than a phone call away.

Daily Information

Daily Diary
Daily information is available from at least three sources: the stock exchange, newspapers, and radio reports. With the exception of one or two items (e.g. trading lists and Commonwealth government loan quotations), the information presented on a daily basis relates to the previous day's trading and announcements. This information is published in the stock exchange's 'Daily Diary' and is available to the public either on an annual subscription basis or through the stock exchange library. Included in this publication is information relating to those shares that have been called 'ex dividend' and 'ex entitlement', those upon which dividends have been declared, and those for which applications have closed. A full round-up of indices from the previous day's trading appears as do a series of reports about various mining and oil ventures. Advice to shareholders from company management as well as notices of meetings also figure. Current takeover offers, new issues pending, and short-term money market rates round out a comprehensive list of sharemarket information.

For those investors not disposed to subscribe to this document, information summaries are available via daily radio reports and newspapers. Stock exchange broadcasts are made daily from radio stations in Adelaide, Brisbane, Hobart, Melbourne, Perth, and Sydney. A full list of these can be found in Appendix C.

Information is also available on a daily basis through newspapers. The extent of the information available differs according to the newspaper. However, as a rule the national dailies tend to supply the most comprehensive information. In our opinion, perhaps the best national daily is the *Australian Financial Review*. Besides much statistical information on share prices, fixed-term securities, and indices movements, it also contains a wealth of information on the state of the market in general and on individual companies within the market.

Weekly Information

Weekly Diary
Weekly information is available from several sources, including some of those already mentioned, e.g. newspapers. Perhaps the most comprehensive weekly summary, however, is that published by the stock exchange. Two publications stand out. These are the *Weekly Dividends, Issues and Offers* publication and the *Weekly Diary*, which are published separately by the stock exchange. Included in the former are a list of dividends declared in the last week, the interest rates on notes and debentures, new issues pending, current takeover offers, and a list of calls made by various companies.

The 'Weekly Diary' includes information relevant to the following week. There are details on shares that will be called 'ex dividend' as well as those shares on which a dividend is payable next week. There are comments in the same vein relating to notes and debentures. Information is also available in respect of those shares on which applications have closed and those that will be traded 'ex bonus', 'ex rights', or 'ex entitlement' during the next week. A list of annual general meetings to be held on various days of the coming week, together with the venue and time of the meeting, is also supplied.

Another weekly stock exchange publication that may be of interest is that describing the weekly course of sales of fixed-term securities.

Monthly Information

Australian Stock Exchange Journal
Probably the most important source of information about the Australian sharemarket — the *Australian Stock Exchange Journal* — is an invaluable publication. While it presents a wide selection of statistics regarding every listed company, it is concerned mainly with the immediate market position of individual companies. Thus it includes details of the current market price of shares, the high and low prices for shares in the immediate past, and the not so immediate past, as well as highly important details on the volume of shares sold in the previous month. There is also information as to new issues pending, as well as current bonus and rights issues.

The *Australian Stock Exchange Journal* is also probably the best source on the total listings on the Australian stock exchange. In this respect, besides all ordinary securities, it provides details of all the preference shares and convertible securities listed. There are also separate tables showing the dates of conversion and the conversion ratios of these securities. The *Journal* also contains tables of all listed fixed-term securities along with the maturity date and interest component of each. Other regular features include:
   (a) a monthly drilling report
   (b) a report on the options market
   (c) a report on the futures market
   (d) a report on the money market
   (e) an international stockmarket report
   (f) a list of the top 200 companies
   (g) a table of current interest rates and
   (h) information on current takeovers.
All things considered the *Australian Stock Exchange Journal*, at $2.50 per copy, is value for money.

Comparative Analysis
Besides the *Australian Stock Exchange Journal*, the exchange also publishes a series of financial (ratio) information in which inter and intra industry rankings of

companies are made. The work is entitled *Comparative Analysis* and is freely available on an inspection basis, as are all stock exchange publications, from the exchange library.

Annual Information

Stock Exchange Research Handbook
Available to the public at $55 per annum, this publication includes information on about 500 listed companies. Besides a section that provides general information about the stock exchange, also included is information relating to company profit announcements, company profits, and statistics based on company financial data.

Financial and Profitability Study
Published by the stock exchange, this work is based on the monthly publication *Comparative Analysis*. Companies are identified with and ranked within nineteen industry groupings. The study analyses the profitability, growth, and financial structure of a sample of companies, chosen on the basis of their size and market domination.

Company Profit Announcements
Yet another in a comprehensive series of publications released by the stock exchange, *Company Profit Announcements*, includes all listed company preliminary profit announcements up to 30 June. The report is divided into four parts. The first part identifies the industry classification; the second, the largest companies by market capitalization; the third, the largest profit earners; and the fourth, the largest pre-tax loss makers.

Stock Exchange Statex Service
Updated annually, this publication provides a ten-year computer summary of specific companies' financial performance. Data includes balance sheet and profit-and-loss details, key financial ratios, sharemarket perform-

ance, investment returns, and cash flow and sales analysis.

Australian Business Profitability

This is a publication produced by P.A. Consulting Services Pty Ltd. It reviews the previous year's financial results of most medium-to-large Australian companies. The sample varies from year to year, but is based on those companies that have assets in excess of $5 million or pre-tax profit in excess of $500,000.

Measures of company profitability include the return on total assets and the return on shareholders' funds. These measures are produced on an industry, market wide, and company-specific basis. Some comparison is made between the results achieved in Australia with those in other countries, in particular the United States of America.

This publication is currently available at an annual subscription of $195.

Jobson Year Book

Although there are a number of annual publications providing information on companies, perhaps the one giving the most comprehensive financial information is the *Jobson Year Book*, in particular the two volumes dealing with public companies and mining companies. Unlike the two previous publications, which are based on samples, the Jobson books include all listed public companies and all listed mining companies, respectively. Although the two publications are not cheap, being $110 and $70 respectively, the wealth of summarized information that they provide is good value for money.

Besides a five-year statistical and financial survey, these publications include a summary of each company's business operations, its directors, managers, auditors, registered office, and capital breakdown. Also supplied is a brief history of the company.

Company Annual and Interim Reports

Another source of information is company annual and interim reports. Every shareholder and debenture-holder is entitled to a copy of these reports. A copy must be lodged with the Corporate Affairs Commission after which it is available for public inspection. Interim reports contain similar information to that in the annual reports, but relate only to the first six months of the financial year. Besides the financial and statistical information in these reports, there are projections on development and future prospects.

Other Publications

Several other annual publications are available but, unlike the three above, do not give summarized statistics based on company financial data. Two of note are *Kompass*, published by Peter Issacsons, and *Business Who's Who*, published by R. G. Riddell Pty Ltd. Both publications include information on company products and services, company management, and parent and affiliate company connections. Also included are the names of the company's bankers and auditors. These two publications constitute excellent supplementary sources.

Periodic Information

Sharebrokers' Newsletters
Most of the larger sharebroking firms send out newsletters to their clients, either at random or at regular intervals. These are usually prepared by the research staff employed by the firm. This practice has increased substantially in recent years. These newsletters are normally up to date and pertinent. Recommendations in respect of purchases will frequently be put forward in these newsletters. Occasionally brokers will advise clients to sell shares. There is an increasing awareness by sharebrokers to advise clients to review their portfolio of investments regularly.

These newsletters will frequently provide interesting information on such matters as new cash and bonus issues, increases or decreases in dividends about to be paid, new listings, takeovers, and general information regarding specific companies and graphs of company and market growth.

Investment Letters

In recent years a proliferation of tip sheets have arrived on the Australian business scene. These include *Australian Money Market Weekly*, *Australian Property Investor*, *Investing Today*, the *Johnson Report*, the *McCabe Letter* and *Your Money Weekly*. Depending on the particular letter, these are available weekly, fortnightly, or monthly. They are primarily available on a subscription basis through the respective consulting firms that are responsible for their publication. They can also be obtained, for perusal purposes only, through the stock exchange library. All are compiled by persons whom one might describe as investment entrepreneurs.

Forecasting Letters

Several banks and individuals publish information forecasting changes in the market. As a rule these are compiled not by investment entrepreneurs but by professional economists. Two of these publications are *Midas* and *Syntec*.

Business Journals

Besides investment and forecasting letters, there exists a number of business journals, which publish information of both a general and specific nature about industries, companies, and securities. These include *Business Review Weekly*, the *Business Bulletin*, and *Australian Business*. Although they contain little about sharemarket movements, the details provided could well be said to initiate and sometimes explain movements.

Stock Exchange Investment Service

Upon receiving the annual reports of each listed company, the Stock Exchange Research Service produces an annual update or overview of a company's operations and financial performance. Included in this annual update is information in respect of the company's registered office, its board of directors, its operations, its subsidiaries, its consolidated accounts, and its major shareholders. Also included is information regarding dividend payments for the previous year, capital reconstructions, and new issues. These annual updates appear on different coloured paper, each signifying either an industrial or mining and oil company. Blue and buff are used for mining and oil companies, and yellow and green for industrial companies.

Besides this annual service, white sheets are released on a continuous basis as details are available. This service is available on a subscription basis, but for the small investor is readily available in most libraries.

Comment

Obviously, for the new investor, this plethora of information on the sharemarket and related business and economic conditions could prove overwhelming. We advise investors to peruse whatever magazines, news sheets, and so on are held at your public and stock exchange libraries, and then subscribe to those appropriate to the size of their portfolios.

Chapter Eighteen
Dealing with Brokers

As we have pointed out, an investor is unable to deal directly on the sharemarket: he must operate through an accredited broker. Brokers differ greatly in their approach to clients, which reflects their individuality. Some will adopt a relatively 'hard sell' attitude. Others will leave all decisions to the client, without commenting on whether they regard the client's decisions to be good or bad.

Choosing a Broker

Different brokers suit different investors. A potential investor should 'shop around' to find a broker who suits him. A complete listing of accredited brokers can be found at the back of the *Australian Stock Exchange Journal* or a small publication of the Sydney Stock Exchange entitled *Members, Member Firms and Partners*.

Many investors will be highly dependent on brokers to help them decide on investments, requiring them to have a very confidential relationship with a broker. In some respects an investor who relies too heavily on a broker is in an unfortunate position, because very few brokers are willing to make definitive statements about a particular company's prospects. This reluctance is natural, as unpredictability is a characteristic of the market.

Do not believe that once you have opened an account with one broker that you may not deal with a second broker. Some investors may well find it advisable to be a client of more than one broker, particularly if the investor requires large volumes of what might be termed 'specialist stock', such as debenture stock, which may not be available from every broker. He may in such a case find it desirable to employ a broker who specializes in such stock and make use of another broker for general share purchases.

Some investors employ both a small local broker and a city broker. This could be advisable where an investor wants to take up new issues, which may not always be made available to the small brokers. If an investor wants to participate in new issues, he should attempt to become an established customer of one of the larger broking firms who deal in new flotations.

Making the Best Use of a Broker

An investor who has some knowledge of the sharemarket and the specific companies he is interested in will be more able to discuss possible purchases with a broker. If the broker advises against purchase of a particular share, for a reason that the potential investor had not considered, then such advice should be heeded. The broker may well have information that is not generally available.

Never be indecisive with a broker. Much animosity between client and broker has been caused by uncertainty and confusion. To avoid this animosity, give a clear and unequivocal order to a broker once you have made a clear decision. Be clear on the price and the number of shares you want to purchase or sell. It is always advisable to set a specified price, a limit beyond which you will not buy or sell.

You cannot blame your broker if you buy shares that subsequently fall in price. Adopt a rational attitude towards your broker, and remember that even if you have a topline broker, decisions are ultimately yours, and when buying shares you are engaging in a speculative exercise.

If you are a seller, make sure you have your certificates at hand to give to the broker once the sale is made. Make sure that you do not ask him to sell more shares than you have. Do not leave a transfer lying around unsigned. Return it to the broker as soon as possible. If buying, make sure you have the funds available to pay for the shares. Brokers will not and cannot be expected to provide credit to clients.

Appendix A
Brokerage Rates

Prior to 1 April 1984, brokerage charges were fixed. On listed company shares, capital stock, rights to new issues, share options and convertible loan securities, both the buyer and seller could be expected to pay a flat $5 plus,

    2.5 per cent on the first $5000
    2.0 per cent on the first $10,000
    1.5 per cent on the next $35,000
    1.0 per cent on the next $200,000
    0.75 per cent on the next $250,000, and
    0.50 per cent on amounts exceeding $500,000

The net effect of deregulation on small private investors investing less than $25,000 has been to substantially increase brokerage charges. An example may best serve to illustrate what has happened. Assume that an investor wants to trade to the value of $100. Prior to deregulation the investor in our example would have been charged $5 plus 2.5 per cent of $100 (that is, $7.50) giving a rate of 7.5 per cent brokerage. After deregulation, brokerage on this transaction would now cost 35 per cent (nearly five times as much). Also bear in mind that this rate is for one side of a transaction. If you consider a 'round trip', that is, a buy and a sell, brokerage charges would be at least doubled.

This situation arises because, almost to a firm, each broker now charges a flat $35 fee instead of the old $5. Some brokers charge an even higher fixed fee. Their reasoning is simple: in the booming market of the last two years, brokers are not interested in wasting their resources on small trades (unless the trades are for clients who trade frequently) and so they set their brokerage rates to discourage such trades.

To get the average pre-deregulation rate of 2.5 per cent brokerage you must now trade at least $1400. By contrast, most of the large institutional clients of brokerage organisations receive rates of around .70 per cent, nearly four times lower than the best possible rate for small private clients. The only way of small private clients taking advantage of this rate without joining the 'big boys' through one of their managed investment funds is to employ the services of a discount broker such as Pont Securities.

Unfortunately, you don't get something for nothing and in order to achieve this favourable rate you must trade at least $15,000 and in addition you lose all broker ancillary services such as advice and research. In this respect a discount broker is much like a no-frills supermarket with all the inconvenience of small aisles and unpacked products. In the case of the discount broker your product is very much unpacked in the sense that it has no implicit sanctioning of the broker (no brand name). Mind you, if you're a small private investor you may well find yourself getting very little from your broker these days, in which case it may be worth your while to go the discount broking way (assuming you wish to continue doing your own trading).

Which avenue you choose depends crucially on what you think you get by way of valuable advice from your non-discount broker. At all times you must balance the extra costs imposed by brokers against the benefits they offer in terms of expected share returns. At the same time you should bear in mind that gone are the days when you could invest virtually any amount in the market. By force of circumstances, trades of less than $3000 are becoming more and more difficult to execute at favourable rates. Indeed, it has become more and more difficult to find a broker who will even accept the business. Consequently, relative returns on these trades are much less attractive when compared to an investment in some form of managed investment fund, such as a unit trust, where the combined buying power of many investors can secure much lower brokerage charges. In this case we have yet another trade-off: this time between the benefit offered by the lower brokerage rate and the costs which the management of these funds scoop off the top. For amounts of less than $3000, the current advantage rests with the managed investment. However, this could change rapidly if the current boom climate discontinues and brokers are forced to drop their rates to again attract smaller clients.

Appendix B
Glossary of Sharemarket Terms

Not all of the terms in this glossary have been used in the text of this book, but they are commonly used in the publications referred to throughout.

Acid Test Ratio
A measure of financial solvency (also known as quick asset ratio), which is calculated by dividing cash and other assets readily convertible into cash by current liabilities.

All Ordinaries
A term used to describe an index in which all shares on the Exchange are included in the calculation of the index.

Annual Report
The formal financial and financially related statements required by law and issued once a year by a company. Included in this report are four mandatory statements: the balance sheet, the profit-and-loss statement, the directors' report, and the auditors' report.

Assets
Those resources owned or at the disposal of a company or individual.

Auditors' Report
A statement attesting to veracity of information contained in the annual report.

Authorized Capital
This is the amount of funds represented by shares that a company is permitted to issue according to its memorandum of association.

Balance Date
The date, usually 30 June, to which the annual accounts are officially drawn up.

Balance Sheet
Comprising part of the annual report, this statement details the assets owned by an entity, and the ownership interest in these assets of two groups. Firstly, those who hold shares in the entity, and, secondly, those other than shareholders who provide capital or credit to the entity.

Bear Market
A market in which share prices are declining.

Bid
The price at which an investor is willing to buy shares.

Blue Chip Investment
A term used to designate a company known for the quality and wide acceptance of its product or services, and for its ability to make money and pay dividends.

Bond
A document upon which the details of a loan made to a government or semi-government body are recorded. It usually involves a fixed rate of interest and a fixed price period.

Bonus Dividend
An additional dividend paid to shareholders over and above what they would normally expect to receive. It is normally given by a company to commemorate some event such as a centenary or the making of an exceptionally large profit.

Bonus Increment
The margin between the take-up price of a new issue as against the price of the same company's shares on the market.

Bonus Issue
The issue of shares free of charge to existing shareholders, usually in a predetermined ratio, e.g. one bonus share for every three already held.

Books Closing Date
The date on which a company closes its books to determine those shareholders entitled to a dividend, new issue, etc.

Broker
One who handles orders to buy and sell shares, fixed-term and other securities for a commission.

Brokerage
The commission a broker receives for handling orders to buy and sell shares, fixed term and other securities.

Bull Market
A market in which share prices are rising.

Call
The amount that remains to be paid on a particular share before it becomes fully paid. *See* Contributing Shares.

Capital
The amount of funds a company has in the form of shares.

Capital Gain
A gain that accrues to an investor when his securities increase in value over and above what he paid for them.

Cash Issue
The issue of shares for a cash consideration.

Closing Price
The price quoted on shares at the close of a day's trading on the stock exchange.

Contract Note
Document sent by a broker to a client, recording information in respect of a purchase or sale, e.g. price of shares and brokerage.

Contributing Shares
Shares that are not fully paid.

Convertible Note
A loan made to a company at a fixed rate of interest, which will either be redeemed for cash by the company or converted into ordinary shares on or within specified dates.

Cum
Meaning 'with', hence 'cum dividend', 'cum rights'. Following the announcement of a dividend or rights issue, shares will be traded for a period, entitling the buyer to the dividend (when it is paid) or rights for new shares when the new issue occurs. Shares traded during this time will tend to rise somewhat in price. After the specified period the shares will become 'ex dividend' and 'ex rights'.

Current Assets
Cash and items that are expected to be turned into cash (inventories, accounts receivable) within twelve months of a balance sheet date.

Current Liabilities
Debts of a company payable within one year of a balance sheet date.

Current Ratio
An accounting term used to describe a means of comparison between current assets and current liabilities.

Debenture
A loan (secured by a charge over a company's assets) made to a company for a fixed rate of interest over a fixed period of time. Part of a group of securities known as fixed-term securities.

Deferred (dd)
Shares quoted (dd) are associated with companies undergoing capital reconstruction where shareholders having surrendered old scrip are awaiting new scrip (share certificates).

(Del)
Shares quoted (del) refer to a new issue for which scrip has not yet been issued.

Director
A person elected by shareholders to establish company policies. One such policy relates to the amount, if any, of dividends that will be paid.

Directors' Report
A statement, comprising part of the company's annual report, that describes past and likely future performance from the directors' viewpoint. It appears in narrative form.

Discount
The amount by which a security is traded below its par value.

Diversification
The spreading of investment funds between investments to minimize the effects of risk and uncertainty. A company may also diversify its products.

Dividend
Amount paid to shareholders as interest on their investment. It is based on a company's profitability, and usually expressed on a per share basis.

Dividend Cover
The number of times dividend payout is covered by the profit available to ordinary shareholders.

Dividend Rate
The dividend paid to shareholders shown as a percentage of the par value of a share.

Dividend Yield
The dividend paid per share (DPS) shown as a percentage of the latest sale price of a share.

Earnings Per Share (EPS)
The net profit of a company less the interest commitment to preference shareholders divided by the total number of ordinary shares issued.

Earnings Yield
Earnings per share as a percentage of the latest sale price of a share. Often rearranged as the price/earnings (P/E) ratio.

Efficient Market
Term used to describe a market in which all information is fully reflected in the price of a share on the market.

Entitlement Issue
A method of raising capital where existing shareholders may buy new shares at below market prices. The entitlement cannot be sold or transferred. Frequently used by mining and oil companies to raise funds.

Equity
Ownership interest.

Ex
Meaning 'without', hence 'ex dividend' and 'ex entitlement'. The use of the term indicates that shares are being traded without the current dividend or the current entitlement. The opposite of 'cum'.

Ex Date
The date on which shares change from being 'cum' to 'ex', usually the fifth business day prior to and including the book closing date.

Ex Poste
Relating to the past, that which has gone before.

Face Value
The nominal or par value of a share. Indicates the standard unit in cents of a company's share. Bears no relation to market price.

Float (Flotation)
Describes the raising of initial capital by public subscription to securities.

Fixed Assets
Assets that are expected to contribute to the income earned by a business during more than one year.

Fully Paid Shares
Shares upon which the full amount of the initial contract price has been received.

Fundamental Analysis
Analysis of a company based on the calculation of ratios, themselves based on past information in respect to a company's profitability and solvency.

Gilt-edged
Securities noted for their stability.

Growth Stock
Shares that provide the opportunity for a capital gain that is above average.

Intangible Assets
Assets that have little or no physical existence, e.g. patents, goodwill.

Institutional Investor
An organization, the primary purpose of which is to invest its own assets or those held in trust by it for others. The term includes pension funds and insurance companies.

Interim Dividend
A dividend paid during a year representing a return based on the previous six months' financial performance and the outlook for the future.

Issued Capital
That part of authorized capital that has been taken up by the public.

Limit Order
An order of shares in which the buyer places a limit on the price he is prepared to pay for a share.

Market Capitalization
A technique used to rank the size of firms. Calculated by multiplying the number of issued shares of a company by the latest sale price of its shares.

Market Order
Term applying to an order of shares to be executed at the best possible price, usually at the broker's discretion.

Market Price
The prevailing price around which a security is bought and sold.

Marketable Parcel
The minimum number of shares at a certain price that can be traded. The marketable parcel for 50 cent and $1 shares is 500 and 100 shares, respectively.

Minority Interest
Describes the interests of those shareholders in a company who do not have the majority of the voting rights.

Company law has, in recent times, taken steps to protect the rights and interests of minority shareholders, to prevent oppression by the majority.

Net Assets
Total assets less total liabilities.

Net Tangible Asset Backing (NTAB)
A frequently quoted company statistic describing the net assets owned by shareholders.

Net Tangible Assets
Total assets less intangible assets.

No Liability
Term used to describe a company in which the shareholders are not obliged to pay calls on their shares. Usually applies to mining companies.

Nominal Capital
The authorized capital of a company.

Non-Renounceable Issue
Describes an issue of shares that cannot be sold or transferred. An entitlement issue is always non-renounceable.

Odd Lot
Shares in numbers that do not constitute marketable parcels.

Offer
The price at which an investor is willing to sell shares.

Official List
A list of companies granted quotation on the stock exchange.

Opening Prices
The prices quoted on shares at the official opening of a day's trading on the stock exchange.

Option
Describes the right attached to a share issue that permits the purchaser to take up further shares at some future date at a fixed price. Options may be traded on the market.

Par Value
The nominal or face value of a security, determined by a company, and displayed on the share certificate.

Pari Passu
Meaning 'equal in every respect'. Term usually applied to a particular class of shares to indicate that they carry equal voting and dividend rights.

Placement
The investment of funds, usually in large amounts, in particular securities.

Points
A measure used to indicate changes in the stock exchange indices. See chapter 12 for an explanation of how indices are calculated.

Portfolio
Comprises the total selection of companies that an investor has placed funds in.

Preference Share
Unit of capital with prior rights to dividends and sometimes capital repayment over ordinary shareholders.

Premium
The margin between the par value of a share and the market value.

Price/Earnings Ratio (P/E ratio)
Describes the relationship between the market price of a share and earnings per share.

Prospectus
A document prepared by a company setting out the terms and conditions associated with a new issue of its securities.

Proxy
Authority, in writing, to vote on behalf of another shareholder at a company meeting.

Quotation
Describes the exercise of listing the current buying and selling prices of a share or shares.

Rally
Describes a period when shares rise after a period of declining prices.

Rights Issue
An issue of capital in which shares are offered to existing shareholders, in predetermined ratios, below their market price. Rights are tradeable on the market.

Scrip
Another term for a share certificate.

Securities
Types of investments offered by companies or government authorities, e.g. shares, debentures, bonds, notes.

Share Certificate
An official record of the equity of a particular shareholder in a company. Must be relinquished when shares are sold.

Shareholders' Funds
Describes the sum of all shareholder equity in a company.

Share Split
An action whereby, in an effort to make its shares more tradeable, companies divide their capital into smaller units. For example, change from $1 to 50 cent shares.

Stags
Persons who buy shares with the intention of immediately reselling them and making a quick profit.

Stocks
Term used interchangeably with 'shares': American in origin.

Stockbroker
Similar origin to above. Used interchangeably with 'sharebroker'.

Stockmarket
Similar origin to 'stocks'. Used interchangeably with 'sharemarket'.

Takeover
An action in which one company buys sufficient shares of another company in order to take over the management of its operations.

Trustee Investment
Certain investments are so classified, as being those that trustees (people who manage money on behalf of others) are entitled to invest in. These include government securities and the securities of some public companies.

Ultra Vires
A legal term to describe a company that conducts operations in areas not authorized by its memorandum and articles of association. Lit. outside the law.

Underwriter
Organization or person who, for a commission, guarantees full subscription to a new issue of shares. Part of the agreement entails the underwriter buying any unsold shares.

Unsecured Note
A fixed-interest security of the same nature as a debenture, except for the fact that it is not secured by a charge over company assets.

Yield
Earnings, dividends, or interest paid by a company expressed as a percentage of the current market price of a share.

Appendix C

Radio Australia Broadcasts

BUSINESS REPORT

AET	GMT	Target Area	Bands
1820	0820	Asia	13, 16 metre bands
		Pacific	19, 25, 31, 49 metre bands
		UK/E	25, 31 metre bands
2220	1220	Asia	25, 31 metre bands
		Pacific	49 metre bands
		Nth. America	31 metre bands
0020	1420	Asia	25, 31 metre bands
		Pacific	49 metre bands
0220	1620	Asia	25, 31, 49 metre bands
		Pacific	49 metre bands
0420	1820	Pacific	16, 25, 31, 49 metre bands
		UK/E	13 metre bands
0620	2020	Pacific	16, 25, 31 metre bands
0820	2220	Asia	13, 25, 49 metre bands
		Pacific	16, 19 metre bands
1020	0020	Asia	13, 19 metre bands
		Pacific	16, 19 metre bands

AET — Australian Eastern Time
GMT — Greenwich Mean Time

Stock Exchange Broadcasts

Broadcasts for each capital city (excluding Canberra) may be received on the following stations or telephone lines:

ADELAIDE	Radio	5CL: 1.15 p.m. & 6.23 p.m. Regionals 1.15 p.m. & 6.15 p.m. 5AA: 7.35 a.m. & 6.05 p.m. Tuesday to Friday. 7.50 a.m. on Saturdays.
	Telephone	11510 — Price changes at 11.00 a.m. & 3.45 p.m.
BRISBANE	Radio	4QG & relay stations (VL09 & VLM4 Short-Wave): 1.15. 4GG 1.05 — 4BH 12.50.
	Telephone	1193 — Price changes at 11.45 a.m., 1.15, 3.45 p.m.
HOBART	Radio	7ZL, 7NT, 7QN: 1.15
	Telephone	1193 — Price changes at 9.30 a.m., 11.00 a.m., 12.50, 3.45 p.m.
MELBOURNE	Radio	3AR, 3GI, 3WB, 3WL and VLH15: 1.45, 7ZR (Hobart), VLR9: 1.15 p.m., 5.58 p.m.
	Telephone	Industrials 11513 Mining & Oil A-H 11511 Mining & Oil I-Z 11517 Price changes are at 9.30 a.m., 11.00 a.m., 1.00 p.m. and 4.00 p.m.
PERTH	Radio	6WN & Regionals — 1.18 p.m. 6GE, 6.00 a.m., 6VA, 6WB & BY, 6MD — between 4.00 p.m. & 5.00 p.m. 6PR — 5.25 p.m. 6KY — 5.30 p.m.
	Telephone	11510 — Price changes 11.00 a.m. & 4.00 p.m.
SYDNEY	Radio	2FC & Regionals, also VL1: 1.15, 5.58 p.m. 2CH — 5.35 p.m.
	Telephone	Mining 11511 Oil 11512 Industrials — A-H 11513 Industrials — I-Z 11515 Price changes at 9.30, 11.00 a.m., 12.00 noon, 2.30, 3.00, 3.30 p.m.